T0128476

DAVID AND MICHELANGELO

HEART AND STONE

By Dr. Stephen Harrison
And Richard Huizinga

WESTBOW
PRESS®
A DIVISION OF THOMAS NELSON
& ZONDERVAN

WestBow Press books may be ordered through booksellers or by contacting:

WestBow Press
A Division of Thomas Nelson & Zondervan
1663 Liberty Drive
Bloomington, IN 47403
www.westbowpress.com
1 (866) 928-1240

ISBN: 978-1-9736-4655-6 (sc)
ISBN: 978-1-9736-4654-9 (hc)
ISBN: 978-1-9736-4656-3 (e)

Library of Congress Control Number: 2018913905

Print information available on the last page.

WestBow Press rev. date: 02/13/2019

CONTENTS

What did David's best friend and his favorite
women have in common?
The man who kills wild animals and giants leaves
the women defenseless behind Absalom, Tamar,
Amnon... all in the family
What is David really upset about in the family
affair?
David's reactionary position after skipping a family
party

A widow's only son
God... no illegitimate son to reign at this time
God's reputation - it's one thing to damage yours,
but quite another for mine
Absalom – just because I let you come back home
doesn't mean I have to talk to you
Shimei – just because I let an offense pass once
doesn't mean that is forever
Nabal – I was only asking for provisions, but while
I am at it I will take your life and wife
Joab – this is what I get for giving you victories and
defeating your enemies
Michal – this is what I get for saving your life and
trying to get you to be decent

David and Goliath . . . no booty, no fight
Medically speaking how does Bathsheba get pregnant?
What is the difference between the morning after
verses the after mourning?
Abigail – the first attractive wife of another that
David takes

Foreword

The examination of a person's life, as that which is captured in a marble statue against the totality of that same person's life, creates a fascinating exercise of comparison and contrast. If the statue is one of the most famous in history and the subject is, literally, of biblical proportions, the exercise reaches something much deeper and meaningful. When the study is developed by two who has been trained to closely examine the human form and also have a personal history of years sitting in a church pew interpreting the Biblical narrative, the statue can appear to come to life and the hero of the Hebrew Bible can appear at times to be as cold as stone.

The portrayal of David utilizes the recurring biblical theme of an individual considered the least likely person to fulfill God's purposes yet still considered a figure "after God's own heart". Dr. Harrison and Mr. Huizinga's examination of what it means to be an individual "after God's own heart", as applied to relationships, leadership, and devotion to God, recognizes that the image and likeness of God which resides within humans is still bound by the human experience, complete with insecurity, ambition, and lust. Michelangelo's representation of David may appear to represent the latter, but their adept inquiry gives pause to the comparison.

Their analysis is reminiscent of the New Testament writer, the apostle Paul, whose life paralleled the same recurring theme as David's. Paul captured the contrast within himself, as he wrote the Philippians, "...to live in Christ", and acknowledge to the Romans that, "I do not understand my own actions. For I do not do what I want, but I do the very thing I hate."

Each of us can benefit from the exercise of comparing and contrasting what it means to be a person after God's own heart yet chiseled in human form. Dr. Harrison's and Mr. Huizinga's informed study and reflection provide the impetus and examination guide for us to consider our motives and consequential actions. Our personal narratives, unlike David's, are most likely not unfolding while a nation is being built. Like David, however, we attempt to build lives that fulfill that to which we have been called, in spirit of our human frailties. David and Michelangelo: Heart and Stone is a pertinent reminder that it appears God chooses those who are frail with the intent purpose to eliminate doubt as to whose power is ultimately at work in the world.

Reverend Doctor David Smazik

Preface

The life of David contains three major themes in most people's minds, much like a three act play. There is the story of Goliath, next the Psalms, especially the 23rd Psalm, and finally the story of Bathsheba. Michelangelo captures images of all these historical accounts in his statue of David. He depicts the tension and calm of David simultaneously as he prepares to fight Goliath. The calm repose instantly makes us recall the serenity of the 23rd Psalm. Finally, he is exposed just as he ultimately was in the Bathsheba affair and stripped to the core as the court historian did for antiquity. In the first 2 instances David appears to reflect the Heart of God, a state that seems to elude him in later stories. The story of the conquering of Goliath comes fairly early in the adult life of David, a first reference to the heart of God. This event displays so clearly a focus on mission and country; indeed we see the humble shepherd boy stepping back from what has already been a successful military venture earlier and being the humble servant for his older brothers. Yet he is confident because God has been with him and will continue to do so.

The Psalms are a mixture which reflects the turmoil of David's life in competition with the tranquility. The tranquility manifests in the quintessential expression in Psalm 23. We want this to be the heart of God because it represents both strength and tranquility again.

Meanwhile the tension in his life will produce a number of Psalms that express frustration and a sense of loss. Perhaps we, like David, cannot get that tranquility without the tension, though one must wonder if we have to go through such great self inflicted tragedy in order to get the other side of tranquility.

Certainly the story of David and Bathsheba is the apex of self inflicted tension and turmoil rooted in deceit. Furthermore it appears the more one reads the story that there is more than a fair chance that both parties calculated the affair. The reality is that as much as we would like to believe that this affair is an isolated event in the life of David, unfortunately it seems representative of a pervasive pattern for his life as a King who rules by deceit, and a man who fails as a father and husband. David may well pay a price here and repent dearly, but he will continue the type of behavior that disrupts family and Godly bonds.

We ourselves may struggle when we try hard to invoke the Christ symbolism in David. How can we see Christ as David, a successful warrior king who does whatever he wants with the power, whatever he wants with women, and whatever he wants with his friends, even ruining those most loyal? On the other hand if we return to the humble image of trust in the 23rd Psalm, we may also discover that image in ourselves. Michelangelo can indeed bring out the best in David, but God can bring out something even more powerful and miraculous in us all if we simply recognize our humble role.

Introduction

- David's statue of stone versus David's stature and heart.
- The dominating warrior hero of the right brain versus the peaceful, soothing, Psalmist of the left brain.
- Samuel's warning. . .Descriptive or predictive.
- David's many roles, the shepherd boy, the priestly king and sometimes a little bit crazy.
- David's body parts, every perspective matters.
- David versus Goliath, cocky brat versus brave young man.
- "I was only asking a question"
- How quickly people forget a hero.

David has been immortalized for us for many centuries, through many means and for many reasons. David captures the best of God's spirit, combined with the classic features of the heroic, but mortal man. He is, after all, a man after God's own heart, as we read in First Samuel 13:14. His human traits are magnified to such epic proportions that we must stretch our imaginations in order to come up with adequate superlatives. He is at the same time a handsome and yet capable and distinguished warrior. His victory over Goliath is no fluke and not necessarily miraculous no matter how much God may have been behind him. He is equally artistic and gifted in music, both in instrumentation and creative song writing. To capture even a portion of this larger than life legend takes a gifted artist several years to create a masterpiece worthy of such representation.

Indeed sometimes it almost takes one legend to represent another. In this case, Michelangelo enters the picture by crafting the most studied sculpture of all time – the immortal statue of David. The statue represents the traditional image of David as we would like to think of him. The scene is one of solitude by David in preparation for the battle to fight the mighty Goliath for the sake of the country's future. Up until that time Goliath had taunted endlessly David's fellow countrymen who feel impotent to respond to his challenge. The statue shows a resolute look in his eye, as he stands unpretentious looking at the enemy. He is stripped down for battle, having discarded the King's own armor as too bulky and prohibitive of movement. David wishes to be forever unrestricted in both his spirit and his body. Indeed his spirit and body are both raw and palpable in this image. Just as there is nothing to detract from this epic figure, so too is there nothing to detract from the image of David that the sculpture seeks to detect. There are no animals to represent his sheep or the flock or the symbolic nature they will serve throughout his kingship. Rather, there is a repose of a nonchalance with his famous sling draped over his left shoulder. This repose suggests a confidence in his immediate engagement, which is contrasted by the bulging veins of his right neck to show the simultaneous tension. It is as though he is quite adept at being able to hide any anxiety over the immediate circumstances to his enemies, even as he wrestles internally with the anxiety that any fighter has before the peak of battle. Michelangelo has captured the solitudinous image of David as seen so frequently in the calmness of the psalmist.

The appendages speak volumes as well. His left foot and leg is rotated as he prepares to meet his target. In fact, the heel is elevated, as though he is ready to take a step. That step may well be the running that is referred to in I Samuel Chapter 17, versus 48 and 49, when he is running to meet Goliath. This is perhaps why he has already discarded the shepherd staff mentioned in First Samuel 17 verse 40. We must allow, though, also just as there are imperfections in our real David, so too are there imperfection in Michelangelo's sculpture along with the missing shepherds and the fact that this very much Jewish young man is uncircumcised. In the statue, David's right hand, which is likely his dominate, is disproportionately larger than his left and is arguably, concealing the one stone that he has in his hand. [see 1 Samuel 17:48-49]. Some disproportionate representation no doubt is intentional, even as our hero had disproportionate traits.

Michelangelo's colossal statue of David is 17 feet tall. This is fitting because we cannot conceive of David without thinking big. We begin by recalling that David kills big giants because he serves a bigger God. He replaces women's adulation because he has bigger conquests. He replaces Saul as king because he has a bigger heart. He writes some really big hits like the 23rd Psalm because he has a big soul. To be sure he makes some big blunders. We can forgive what me might think of as his biggest sin with Bathsheba because he is big and bold to go to God and repent. While there are big consequences of death for that offspring, this is followed by an even bigger reward in the birth of Solomon. But to leave that summary as representative of David's life would be a big mistake. There are many other lessons big and little that we may benefit from in reflection.

It is easy to get caught up in the dominating features of the epic warrior-hero, youth-savior complex. Those features will indeed come out in our story, but there are several more dimensions to our image of David. His left hand is much smaller and more delicate. It represents the right brain and the creative aspect. This is the gifted musician who can play the shepherds harp and write soothing psalms. It is contrasted with the calculating logical side of David's left brain, which may get him into trouble at times. Both the right and left sides of the brain are born out early in David's career, as early as First Samuel 16. In this section King Saul is seeking someone who can have a calming influence upon him and asks for someone who plays the harp. We see in I Samuel 16:18, combining various versions, that David was already considered not only an accomplished harp player, but also handsome, brave, strong, a gifted speaker, with solid judgement, mighty, smart, courageous, valiant, eloquent, articulate, and virtuous. This seems to indeed be the all around man with both left and right brain skills that anyone would find appealing. The circumstances behind this request by King Saul come because Saul has been troubled and depressed since the spirit of the Lord had been tormenting him with depression and fear. God's spirit had indeed been withdrawn from King Saul, because he did not obey God and was impatient trying to take over the priestly role and not having the effective separation of church and state that God wanted still to exist when the people of Israel demanded to have a King over them like other countries. At that very moment God's spirit was bestowed upon David when it is withdrawn from Saul.

Let us turn to the description of the type of king that Samuel described through God's direction that the people of Israel would encounter. "So Samuel told them, deliver God's warning to the people who are asking Him give them a king." He said, "This is the way the kind of king you are talking about operates. So, take your sons and make soldiers of them – chariotry, calvary, infantry, regimented in battalions and squadrons. He'll put some forced labor on his farms, plowing and harvesting and others to make either weapons of war or chariots in which he can ride in luxury. He will put your daughters to work as beauticians, waitresses and cooks. He'll conscript your best fields, vineyards, and orchards and hand them over to his special friends. He'll tax your harvest and vintage to support his extensive bureaucracy. Your prize workers and best animals he will take for his own use. He'll lay a tax on your flocks and you will end up no better than slaves. The day will come when you will cry in desperation because of this king that you want so much for yourselves, but don't expect God to answer." That is the MSG I Samuel 8, versus 10-18.

We must keep in mind that God would not get rid of either King Saul or King David for adhering to this particular description, as God predicted this is what would happen with basically any king. Our purpose here will be to determine in which ways this was accomplished by David and through what various roles he plays. We will also keep ever mindful the notion that God's says that he is a man after his own heart.

Let's look at some of those various roles that David will play in the course of his lifetime. He will indeed be the brave soldier, while at the same time being the creative artist. Like the statue of David, these two items are in a dynamic tension. He is forever the shepherd trying to rescue or protect his flock and taking responsibility for them. Perpetually the concept of shepherding and sheep will be a recognizable role throughout his kingship, including several of his major blunders. He is very loyal to the people symbolized by the sheep at large, but often struggles on an individual basis with those closest to him. For example, he is a champion warrior on the one hand that is missing in action when his best friend is killed in a battle when arguably David could have made a difference for his friend's life. In fact, the warrior David is actually hiding at that very moment. Yet, he has a conscience that gets the better of him when he has the opportunity to kill King Saul on several occasions and justifiably so. However, that conscience restrains him. He is able to console even his mighty enemies such as King Saul who throws spears at him, but arguably there are very few references in which he can console his own family members when they need it most. For example, he is not able to console his daughter Tamar when she is raped; rather his son Absalom was quite troubled about that event. He himself cannot be consoled when Absalom is subsequently killed following the revolt that Absalom performed against David. Strangely David cannot be consoled, at this time even though his son had turned viciously against him. It is as though there is unresolved tension, like the statue. There is a lack of complete forgiveness that goes beyond simply the death of a promising son.

Through all of this David will play many roles in his lifetime and will accentuate various representations of his heart, body, spirit and soul. He will masquerade as a crazy man would. He will use his cunning and deceit against other Kings to protect his own life when this is what it takes for self preservation. He will masquerade as a priest and be accused by those close to him of a perversion that goes beyond the ecclesiastical perversion of wearing priestly clothing all in the same situation. In this situation David is someone who in one way or the other lets it all hang out, but the ultimate expression of his role playing comes when he portrays himself as perfect in the last major speech before he dies. II Samuel Chapter 22, "The Lord has dealt with me according to righteousness; according the cleanness of hands he has rewarded me. For I have kept the ways of the Lord; I am not guilty of turning from my God. All of his laws are before me; I have not turned away from his decrees. I have been blameless before him and have kept myself from sin. The Lord has rewarded me according to my righteousness, according to my cleanness in his site". (II Samuel 22:21-25 NIV). This statement about perfection comes immediately before his egotistical blunder cost seventy thousand of his fellow countrymen their lives. Michelangelo's statue of David is the perfect or ideal representation of David's key features.

We will have occasion to reference various bodily parts and functions in our treatise in order to determine what really represents the heart of God mentioned. We have just seen reference to David's ego, which will surface time and again a classic Freudian sense. Indeed, the bravagado scene in the David and Goliath Story is just one of many instances, as is the David and Bathsheba story. There are other ways to psychologize our understanding of David, such as the more modern Transactional Analysis. In this setting David can be interpreted as often stuck in the perpetual adolescent or pre-adult role represented by a child. On one hand the child like, naivety and dutifulness can be appreciated. On the other hand, there is great frustration with the David we see that has incredibly poor parenting skills. Once again he appears to have no intervention at times when there would be a great desire to have those interventions in any culture or in any kind of society when there is an incestual and deceptive rape. We have alluded to the cunning and deceit in role playing that David is capable of, but arguably his own anointing was inaugurated with a veil of deceit. In I Samuel 16 we have God citing the prophet Samuel who had anointed Saul for mourning too long for Saul after he departed from God's ways. God is looking for a replacement, but Samuel is fearful, "how can I do that, Samuel asked, if Saul hears about it, he will kill me! (I Samuel 16:2 GNB)". God then gives Samuel a plan that will make it appear that Samuel is coming only to offer sacrifices to God himself when in reality this is only part of the mission. The real mission is to elect a new King to replace Saul, which would be David, son of Jesse. Perhaps David would use this example as a pretense for he himself to deceive others throughout his tenure as king. He of course is well aware that Saul had attempted to deceive God and did not get away with it. While there will be violations of God's commandments, David will not seek directly to deceive God during his reign. Eventually Saul bans David from his presence and demotes him, but this strategy only put David in a more favorable view in the public's eye. [I Samuel 18] In First Samuel 15:28-29 we note that Samuel says David was greater than Saul, in terms of ability and stature, etc. Ultimately the people pick up on this and therefore David is banned by Saul. However, this only increases his stature among the people. This is a sign of being irrepressible and perhaps captures some of the heart of God in that sense. The real David will appear, like the statue, both tense and calm, strong and peaceful, lustful and earthy, proud and arrogant, along with being a lousy family man. At least two of his sons will kill their brother while a third rapes his sister. He is a consummate womanizer, who may win women over only to treat them questionably, even after they have saved his life. We will indeed see David's life as we have it recorded, as being framed by women and hormonal conquest, as much as it is by the warrior-hero conquest.

We return momentarily to our sculpture of David and the attention we have given to the appendages. The final two appendages are the phallus and the slingshot. We have already noted the uncircumcised nature, which would have been uncharacteristic for the Jewish hero with David's lineage, but we note that there may be many reasons for this that would include, besides the oversight, the notion of being modest. Modesty may have been part of the rationale behind the relatively small male organ portrayed for David here. This may have been an attempt to express the youthful nature of David, while others might note that the body would divert blood from sexual organs when one is preparing for the fight or flight syndrome. Certainly though, Michelangelo did not capitalize on the key theme of the circumcision that David himself calls attention to on more than one occasion. For example, he belittles Goliath as uncircumcised when asking, who is this uncircumcised Philistine, etc. In addition, when David is to come up with a response to King Saul's challenge before he weds Michal he is to bring the foreskins of one hundred uncircumcised Philistines. Perhaps Michelangelo did not wish to portray the elements of womanizing as so largely defined in David's lifetime. Keep in mind that this is the same individual who will sleep with a woman immediately after she has lost her baby, in order to console her. (II Samuel 12)

The Slingshot, meanwhile, is a reactionary tool with its activity fueled by a preceding tension that is subsequently released. It is the ultimate metaphor for David, as it stands for hidden potency in a potentially overlooked object. Michelangelo effectively sculpts this object right into David's body. It is essentially another appendage like his hands, feet, and phallus. To protect, or to acquire a prey, all of these can be forceful and effective agents. They are deceptive tools, slight in nature, even obscure, with the ability to affect dramatic change or damage. The Slingshot, like David, can do its damage up close or at a distance. This is indeed an appropriate metaphor for David, in that it is common for him to use his weapons, including sex to disable, conquer or destroy what or who stands in his way, only then to distance himself from the women involved, the offspring produced, or the damage incurred. This is despite the fact that he knows he needs the loyalty of those friends, family, and the nation that remain standing in order to perpetuate the kingdom. Why does he withdraw?

Michelangelo has captured the essence of David in his famous sculpture. David is a perfect young male, all his features capture an attractive youth, strength, passion, and a focus on his purpose, which in this case is the elimination of Goliath as a personal and political threat to Israel. Rather than a sword or spear to accomplish his goal, David's weapon of choice is surprise- himself, no weapon except a slingshot. And why not? He had used the slingshot successfully many times before surprising the enemies of his herd with a well placed stone followed by the kill, if necessary, to eliminate the aggressor's threat.

The physical and emotional attributes of the sculpture, including the slingshot, portend all the virtues and actions that will make up David's life.

David will emerge from this encounter with Goliath as an immediate hero, followed by a call to be the King and Defender of Israel. His attractive youth, his fearless and aggressive nature, his use of surprise as a tactic will serve his purposes well in war, political battles and his personal life. On his way to becoming King and as King, David's attractive physical and emotional features, his success in war, his status as a powerful leader and his sexuality will provide success and allow him to get what he wants. David's weapons will change, his enemies will no longer be animals, his passionate focus will many times shift from war to power games and sex. And he will learn to use deceit as a new tactic. But the goal remains the same-win by eliminating the obstacles and enjoying the pleasure of success. To be sure. God's approval is part of the reward, but carnal and political rewards are an equally powerful draw.

David will come to epitomize all of this and then some. He will indeed take those sons and turn them into killing machines. He will in the next breath chastise them for killing his enemies, and sometimes even have them killed for doing what appears to be a soldier's duty. He will take those daughters, as mentioned in the scriptures, but will also take grown women who are married to others and have them for his wife and sexual outlet. Indeed the life of David will be framed by his relationships with women. These women don't necessarily have to be his wife. The process may go beyond the familiar story of Bathsheba, but in fact, the hormones of

David will be interwoven throughout key parts of his life, as well as framing his rise to fame and the heralding of his death.

Let us return to our sculpture of David. Once again, we see the sculpture of David as a classic representation of diverse proportions. On one hand David is poised and seems calm and relaxed for whatever comes. On the other hand, he has raised his left leg and his left heel as though he is getting ready to take his first step. This is the first step of running that is mentioned in I Samuel 17:48-49. He will need to take a minimum of 3 steps, but either way a generally odd number and likely a low number in order for him to have an element of surprise and yet stopping in order to steady himself with his left foot forward before he take aim with is right hand. This is indeed the same rapid change that we see in real David's life. In one moment he is posed to fight any battle that God has, the next he is ready to abandon the cause and go into hiding. In fact, seldom in his life will he run towards the battle, as he did when he faced Goliath. Rather, he will run away from family, such as Absalom when he perceives his own life threatened and he will run away from battle when his best friend Jonathan is threatened and ultimately dies in that battle. David is indeed an enigma just like the statue, in which we have a hard time figuring out what the exact motion and motives are.

Let's look again at the story of David and Goliath, which is David's springboard to notoriety. The story that we may often recall is one in which David is playing the role of the youngest child as a mere shepherd boy responding to the request of his father to deliver goods to older brothers at the battle front. We must disillusion ourselves from the notion that David is a naïve and inexperienced fighter. He is already an accomplished soldier, as we read in I Samuel Chapter 16, "One of the servants answered," "I have seen the son of Jesse of Bethlehem who knows how to play the lyre, he is a brave man and a warrior. He speaks well and is a fine looking man. And the Lord is with him." The King James Version notes he is a mighty valiant man and man of war already. ERV lists him as a good fighter, other versions note he is handsome, brave, strong, of good judgement, well spoken, gifted in words, etc. None of these versions nor even a collective representation can capture though the heart of God, as the Living Bible notes at the end, "What's more he added, the Lord is with him." The heart of God seems to go beyond all these criteria. David has, in fact, by the time he reaches the battlefield where Goliath is taunting, already been anointed the King to replace Saul. This is indeed the David that goes to the battle front to bring food to the older brothers. Of course the older brothers don't appreciate this or its impact. But when David's oldest brother Eliab heard David talking like that, he was angry. "What are you doing around here anyway?" he demanded. "What about the sheep you are supposed to be taking care of? I know what a cocky brat you are; you just want to see the battle!" [I Samuel 17:28 LB] David tries to soften the blow by saying now what have I done? David asked. Can't I even ask a question [I Samuel 17:29 GNB] ERV notes, who did you leave those few sheep with in the desert, as though there were rather limited resources at that. The paucity of the sheep referenced in that version make David's forthcoming speech to King Saul even more plausible as to the length that David would go to for a single sheep. "David said, "I have been a shepherd tending sheep for my father. Whenever a lion or a bear came and took a lamb from the flock, I would go after it and knock it down, and rescue the lamb. If it turned on me I would grab it by the throat, ring its neck, and kill it. Lion or bear it made no difference – I killed it. And I will do the same to the Philistine pig who is taunting the troops of God-Alive. God had delivered me from the teeth of the lion and the claws of the bear, will deliver me from this philistine." I Samuel 17:34-37 MSG. So here we have David's bravagado in the form of the highly developed ego. It is as though God is an afterthought in the story and whose help he better invoke just to be on the safe side. Even then he is not highly motivated to perform the task. It would appear that the motivation that he is missing is in a form of a woman, as we will explore in later chapters.

This is a moment of recognition for David and perhaps respect. He has actually already performed the measures we have noted for which he has received acknowledgment before the trip to the battlefront of Goliath and the Philistines. However, people forget quickly, as perhaps David is realizing through this lack of respect for his former accomplishments. Perhaps this is a seed that is planted in his brain, in which he becomes preoccupied with wanting to have a kingdom that would last forever, as he sees how quickly people's memory can fade, even as a youth who is still very much alive. He has soothed the King's tormented mind yet King Saul does not even recognize him. Furthermore Saul would have to have heard also about his military exploits that were suggested in the prior chapter; but let's see what Saul actually says when David proposes to fight the Philistine, "Don't be ridiculous!", Saul replied. "How can a kid like you fight with a man like him? You are only a boy and he has been in the Army since he was a boy!" [17 verse 33 LB]. Shortly after, David will kill the giant and incite a riot with Israel over the Philistines. Even then though Saul will not know who he is, such that he asks his leading general Abner where he hails from. Whether or not David stripped down to fight to the degree that Michelangelo depicts is a matter of contention, though, certainly not unheard of for battles of that nature. Nonetheless, David recognizes that he cannot step into someone else's clothes or role in the exact way that the other individual would. Hence, he rejects Saul's special armor, sword, etc. as being something too restrictive for the movement that he needs. This is the unpretentious David. He is arguably the David that has been presented to us by David's historian, most likely from his own court. This historian has chosen to show David warts and all.

Michelangelo's David on the other hand represents David as we would like to think of him and remember him, as the eternal youth and hero all in the same moment. When Michelangelo conceived of David, he was said to have begun with a stone (that was previously worked on) in which he simply chipped away everything that wasn't David and left what was. Conversely, the reader of this Treatise is asked to remove their preconceptions of David and see what is left over, after we have chipped away at some of the legend's mystique. Keep in mind that we will perpetually be searching for the image of the heart of God and in particular through his exploits and stories. It may be that it will take a composite to see what that heart really is.

INTRODUCTION QUESTIONS

1. As you look into Michelangelo's David what are the various roles of David that you can see?
2. Do we need to study David from different angles in order to see the whole picture?
3. How does David fulfill Samuel's warning about what a King will be like?
4. Are there seeds of deceit sown in David's anointing that he uses later on?
5. Can the heart of God be seen from any angle looking at David?

CHAPTER 1
LOYALTY AND FAMILY MATTERS

- David, don't mess with his animals or God's destiny.
- David. . . It is not my duty to kill a wicked and wayward King.
- I love my best friend, but don't ask me to die for him.
- What did David's best friend and his favorite women have in common?
- The man who kills wild animals and giants leaves the women defenseless behind.
- Absalom, Tamar, Amnon. . . all in the family.
- What is David really upset about in the family affair?
- David's reactionary position after skipping a family party.

As we chip away at our image of David we find that some traits are enduring. At the end of the day, at the end of the reign, at the end of his life, David seems to be incredibly loyal. That loyalty appears in various expressions, to his family, his flock, his people and ultimately to God. Perhaps this is a portion of the heart that God refers to when he says David is a man after his own heart in I Samuel 13:14. The man who rescues sheep from the mouths of lions and bears does not give up easily when something is in his charge. Along with this is a deep seeded belief in the destiny that is ordained by God. The supreme reflection of that belief comes when he refused to take advantage of the several opportunities he has to kill King Saul. Even before these opportunities he risks his life when he tries to console King Saul by playing his musical instrument, only to have the King throw spears at his head. Even while Saul pursues David with the intent of killing him, David will not move himself to inflict harm to the Lord's anointed. If it is meant to be, then the God who helped him with Goliath will make it happen. God will take care of things in his own way and in his own time.

David appears to be rewarded for that way of thinking and for that faith. After all, he becomes King by being patient and letting events unfold according to the plan that is literally divinely ordained. David does not need to intervene to any great extent. After all, God will take care of things. Two times Saul will be within inches of losing his life while David is in his vicinity. David's conscience and refusal to lay a hand on God's anointed will stop him from doing so. Ultimately Saul will self destruct when the final battle is closing in on him and he will kill himself. The only remaining question about loyalty is where David is in the picture. David the mighty warrior of God who has beaten the Philistines badly before and will route them again later, is fearful for his own life and is hiding. This is despite the fact that his best friend Jonathan dies in that battle because of the risk, which outcome arguably would have been different had David been there.

Still, there does not seem to be much question about the bond between Jonathan and that loyalty, beyond even death. This bond seems to be special from the beginning. At Jonathan's funeral David declares that he loved Jonathan more than anyone and we know how much he loved women, II Samuel 1:26. This love or respect was evident at first sight: When David had finished speaking to Saul, the soul of Jonathan was with the soul of David, and Jonathan loved him as his own soul. Saul took him that day and would not let him return to his father's house. Then, Jonathan made a covenant with David because he loved him as his own soul. Jonathan stripped himself of the robe he was wearing and gave it to David and his armor, even his sword, his bow and his belt. I Samuel 18:1-4. Meanwhile, David becomes a successful and mighty warrior and somewhat of a threat to Saul and his kingdom because of his popularity. Saul makes plans to kill David, but Jonathan tips him off to that scheme. After other attempts of reconciliation between David and Saul, Saul planned to kill David. Jonathan warned David and they met in secret. When Jonathan goes to defend David, he has a swearing insult hurled at him: "You son of a slut! Don't you think I know that you're in cahoots with the son of Jesse, disgracing both you and your mother? For as long as the son of Jesse is walking around free on this earth, your future in this kingdom is at risk. Now go get him. Bring him here. From this moment, he's as good as dead! [1 Samuel 20:30 MSG].

Later that night an upset Jonathan meets with David for the final time and they make a pledge that shall be honored between them forever, including their descendents. David appears to hold to his pledge long after Jonathan is gone. Nowhere else does he share this much earthly love and loyalty. I am not proposing anything else be read into this relationship other than it appeared to be a lot more of a commitment than any relationship he had with a woman. Jonathan risks his family connection and even the kingship in his connection with David. He will deceive family to protect David while David will ultimately forsake the battle that predictably kills Jonathan. However, David will never love a woman the way he loved Jonathan. Arguably that premature loss incites David to desire a "forever clause". More on that later.

For now we will take a brief glimpse at the types of women that David went for and see that they have in common with Jonathan, a source of power. What other types of woman does David like? We do not have many physical descriptions of course of these women, but what we do have suggests that he liked beauty and shapeliness. In Psalm 144 which is attributed to David as prayer for victory and prosperity we read his description of the ideal woman. "Our daughters, like carved columns, shapely as those of the temple." [New American Bible] In the Douay-Rheims version the daughters are described as, "decked out." The description of Abigail in First Samuel 25, The American Standard Version, has that she is of a beautiful countenance. The Good News Bible and other versions note that she was both beautiful and intelligent while the Message lists her as good looking as well as intelligent. Indeed Abigail is shrewd and cunning. She applies flattery and appeals to David's ego, by among other things, noting he will do no wrong and that his kingdom will last forever. This cunning style is seen elsewhere in David's attraction for women. Certainly, Michal had a fair amount of this cunning in that she protected David and provided him with the means of escape when he was under pursuit.

We can see an argument can be made that Bathsheba was equally cunning herself in plotting out the strategy to ensnare the King. More on this later.

Many of David's wives share some features of having connection with power and men of power. As we noted, two have been connected with powerful individuals who have been wives to other men, such as Uriah and Nabal. At least two of his wives have been daughters of kings, including Michal. David seems to be attracted to this level of power, intelligence, shrewdness, etc. and not even troubled if the women have belonged to someone else first. However, once there is evidence that the women have been used by other men after they have been in David's possession, he appears to have very little to do with them. Such is very clearly the story of ten of his wives/ concubines whom he left behind when he fled Jerusalem, only to have them be despoiled by Absalom. Subsequent to that David had no relations with them. This also appears to be the case of Michal who was given away by King Saul even after she had married David only to be ultimately returned. However, following that return there is no indication that he had relations with her.

What about David's loyalty and involvement with his own family? Again, we are left with a handful of stories so we have no choice but to take those as illustrative of the challenges that David faced. The story of Absalom is where David takes his non-interventional strategy to the max. This strategy seems to be combined with the belief that God will bless David's kingdom through eternity. The ultimate challenge to this is when Amnon rapes his half sister Tamar. Absalom is the full brother to Tamar. On the one hand he does not want to disturb the king too much on this, or the divine right of kings and their heirs to take certain liberties. We are told that David did not want to say anything in order to minimize saying anything to upset Amnon: "King David heard the news and became very angry, but he did not want to say anything to upset Amnon because he loved him since he was his first born son." [II Samuel 13:21 ERV] David is paralyzed to intervene. Indeed to do so would be stepping in on God's territory potentially God's seed for a future king. Indeed it would be stepping in on God's territory and in more than one way. David has already by this time shown a belief that punishment is to be exacted by God, not by man. God will make Amnon pay for this sin, as indeed it is a sin.

About the best we can say is that not interfering with God's discipline is what David seems to be rationalizing here. The worst is that David sees the act of incestual rape as the divine right of kings. As such, it is merely an extension of what Samuel warned the people of Israel when they wanted to have a king. He said, "This is what the king who will reign over you will do: He will take your sons and make them serve with his chariots and horses, and they will run in front of his chariots." Some he will assign to be commanders of thousands and commanders of fifties, and others to plow his ground and reap his harvest, and still others to make weapons of war and equipment for his chariots. He will take your daughters to be perfumers and cooks and bakers. He will take the best of your fields and vineyards and olive groves and give them to his attendants. He will take a tenth of your grain and of your vintage and give it to his officials and attendants. Your menservants and maidservants and the best of your cattle and donkeys he will take for his own use." [II Samuel 8:11-16 NIV] This lengthy passage is repeated to him both as a curse and warning to the people of Israel, yet literally it is a free reign invitation to the King of Israel to do as he pleases with men, women and resources. Of course, David has set the example by not only taking young and single women, but also married women if they are attractive, and their husband are not around, and if those husbands can be disposed of if need be. Yes, David has not only disposable income and resources, but also has disposable men and women. Uriah has been asked to run before the chariots and lead the troops into battle. Tamar will meanwhile cook for the man who is in line to be king and make perfumes that make her all the more desirous. Why would Amnon think any differently than he did under such circumstances. Amnon is only following the lead when he makes a sexist request to David that his half sister be allowed to help Amnon when he feigns a sickness. How could King David deny him. And yet, how can a king such as David not imagine what might happen next when two young people are alone in the bedroom under those circumstances. David is after all the king of imagination and deceit himself. Is it not too much for a king who pretends to be crazy to think that one of his sons might pretend to be sick in order to have a little intimacy. And we need to be clear about this. It is about a little sex and not about a commitment after the event. Tamar even intrigues Amnon to implore the king to see if they could get married. She rightly calls out the usual consequences of the crime with shame and being called a fool, but it is not enough.

Amnon may well have banked on the king doing nothing. Absalom appears to have figured out the same thing. He makes that seemly, even stronger, sexist remark in II Samuel 13:20. "Is it true that Amnon raped you? Don't be upset since it is all in the family anyway. It is not anything to worry about!" [LB] In The Message we read her brother Absalom said to her, "has your brother Amnon had his way with you? No my dear sister let's keep it quiet, a family matter. He is after all your brother, don't take this so hard!" [II Samuel 13:20]

As if the whole process is not twisted enough already, the word filters up to King David: "King David heard the whole story and was enraged, but he didn't discipline Amnon... Absalom quit speaking to Amnon-not a word, whether good or bad-because he hated him for violating his sister Tamar." [II Samuel 13:21 MSG]. How angry is very angry? After all, David's anger was not followed up by any punishment or consequences. Furthermore, what exactly was David angry about? Let us explore some possibilities.

1. While the rape seems to the obvious answer we must keep in mind that Tamar herself viewed the post rape rejection as her worst consequence of the whole event. But, David does not force a marriage. Is this some of the misplaced understanding that kings don't punish other potential kings because that is God's domain. If God has ordained a king in his family to be king forever then can even the King punish someone who could be potentially king some day, especially if the King is following the interpretation of being King as predicted by Samuel and quoted earlier?

2. David is upset because he was pulled into the plot to seduce Tamar. David's nephew gives the way that Tamar can be seduced: Here is what you do said Jonadab, "go to bed and pretend you are sick. When your father David comes to visit you say have my sister Tamar come and prepare some supper for me here where I can watch her and she can feed me. [II Samuel 13:5 MSG] In this scheme David is upset with Amnon more than the rape itself because he was drug into it.

3. David is upset with himself. In this situation he is upset with himself because he did not see coming what should have been obvious to a man of hormones. In every available version Amnon is very clear – he wants to watch his half sister while she prepares the food. This we doubt is because he wants to make sure she is really fixing it, or because he suspects somebody else might poison him. This is pure and simple psychological foreplay and the man who watches beautiful women from the rooftop should know this. Then, of course, Amnon spells out for David that after Tamar has prepared his meal he wants to eat it from her hands. Jonadab said to Amnon, "go to bed, pretend you are sick. Then your father will come to see you." Tell him, "please let my sister Tamar come in and give me food to eat let her make the food in front of me. Then I will see and eat it from her hand." So, Amnon laid down in bed and pretended to be sick. David came in to see Amnon. He said to King David, "please let my sister Tamar come in, let her make two cakes for me while I watch and then I can eat from her hands." [II Samuel 13:5-6 ERV]

4. David is not upset about the rape, but the fact that Amnon declined to ask the king, that is David, for permission to marry Tamar, as she herself requested.

5. Same as above, but in this situation he is mad simply because Amnon did not marry Tamar, even without asking.

6. David is upset because Amnon hates Tamar after the event. In this scenario rape and marriage refusal are not so bad, but ignoring the family who is good enough for intimacy once is cause for upset and could not be tolerated. After all, look what David did after the Bathsheba event.

7. David is actually upset with Absalom because he does nothing to vindicate the rape.

8. David is upset with Absalom because Absalom doesn't say anything to Amnon, good or bad: "Absalom began to hate Amnon, Absalom did not say one word good or bad to Amnon, but he hated him because Amnon had raped his sister Tamar." [Second Samuel 13:22 ERV] David can perhaps take love or hate, but not indifference and ignore it.

9. David feels upset and guilty because of the Bathsheba affair and the fact that it was not resolved until the preceding chapter. He did not want to be connected with a sin that he was guilty of perpetuating and inspiring his offspring to sin as they invariably do soon after.

Before jumping to dismiss any of the possibilities keep in mind that David did not punish Absalom. Consider looking for clues in the habits of David, which may give us answers. For example, later in the chapter David tears his robe after he is told that Absalom has murdered all of David's sons. In this scene is David, (1) mourning the loss of children? (2) regretting that he did not punish Amnon? (3) fearful that Absalom will come for him?

Of course the matter is not over. Absalom waits two years and decides to throw a party after the sheep have been sheared. This event is of course a sign that Absalom has been blessed.

Two years is enough to wait for God's intervention and David's for that matter. Absalom invited the whole family, but David politely declines the invitation though his rationale is pretty flimsy. Absalom presses for Amnon to come in David's stead. While David questioned that, he relented eventually.

Accordingly all the potential heirs to the throne do go to Absalom's party. Absalom gets his all in the family revenge by killing Amnon.

Somehow in that ancient culture, news had a faster way of traveling than the royal transportation carrying the rest of the royal heirs: "As they were on their way back to Jerusalem, a report reached David: Absalom has killed all of your sons, not one is left alive!" [II Samuel 13:30 LB] News travels fast, but gossip travels faster when there is a fear factor and dire consequences. Note the redundancy for added emphasis. Before it is established as untrue, David will have ripped off his robe and fallen to the ground. In this distorted family affair the cousin Jonadab who is David's nephew, will tell David not to despair too much because it was only Amnon who was killed by Absalom for revenge leading to the rape of Tamar. Keep in mind the fact that this is the same cousin who set up the plot for the rape to begin with. Knowing that Absalom has committed a crime for which he will be expelled was potentially part of an elaborate scheme to get rid of potential heirs one at a time.

This is just one incident where David is prone to reactionary thinking. David is indeed prone to catastrophic thinking in the most extreme of situations. For example, Absalom has a habit of bringing this catastrophic thinking out of David on two separate occasions. In II Samuel 13 verse 30 we read the quote, "while they were on their way home, David was told: Absalom has killed all your sons-not one of them is left!" [II Samuel 13:30 GNB] Then too the same type of thinking happened again as though messengers know what will get David going. In II Samuel 15:13 we read, a messenger soon arrived in Jerusalem to tell King David, "all Israel has joined Absalom in a conspiracy against you!" In both of these situations David seems to hear what he fears the most, that on the one hand all of his offspring is killed leaving only Absalom to rule on that throne forever, almost as if he had read prophecy much like that out of Shakespeare's Macbeth which has come to fruition. In the second scene it is total negativity that the entire nation has joined Absalom in the conspiracy. While both of these turn out to be extremist, they do motivate David to flee the situation without as much as a consultation from God. Earlier David had been reactionary when he was on the run from King Saul. He takes Goliath's sword and goes to the land of King Achish. But the sword of Goliath is not enough to assuage his fears. Rather than consult God at that time he chooses to act crazy.

In the same chapter that David is angry about Amnon's rape he later mourns the death of Amnon. But, he will get over this before the end of the chapter. What he cannot get over is the absence of his son Absalom. Is that because he senses the mistakes that David himself made earlier? Is it because he cannot fathom losing two heirs over the same event? Is this indeed part of David's preoccupation of having his heirs sit on the throne forever? Is it because he senses the need for reconciliation? We will pick that up in the next section.

CHAPTER 1 QUESTIONS

1. Why is the great warrior David missing in action when his best friend Jonathan dies in battle?
2. What does David not get out of his relationship with women that he does get with Jonathan?
3. Why does David ignore his concubines after he left them behind initially to be put in harm's way?
4. What characteristics of David are present during the Absalom, Tamar, Amnon episode?
5. How is the slingshot the ultimate metaphor for David.

CHAPTER 2
RECONCILIATION AND FORGIVENESS

- A widow's only son.
- God. . .no illegitimate son to reign at this time.
- God's reputation – its one thing to damager yours, but quite another for mine.
- Absalom – just because I let you come back home doesn't mean I have to talk to you.
- Shimei – just because I let an offense pass once doesn't mean that is forever.
- Nabal – I was only asking for provisions, but while I am at it I will take your life and wife.
- Joab – this is what I get for giving you victories and defeating your enemies.
- Michal – this is what I get for saving your life and trying to get you to be decent

Perhaps we might interpret David's wish for reconciliation with Absalom as not simply the resolution to a great family conflict, but an opportunity to practice forgiveness. Is not forgiveness part of what God senses in David as a man after his own heart? In the second scene of Chapter 14 we have another setup that suggests that this forgiveness is what will happen. In a setup not as famous as Nathan's poor man/sheep story that occurs after the Bathsheba incident, David is drawn into the plight of a widow and her only two sons. As the story goes, the widow relates how during the fight with each other that one of her two sons killed the other son. When that happened she noted that the rest of the family demanded that the other son be handed over for execution, which would leave the woman without any means of support and destroy the family line. Let's pick up on David's response to this pretense of a story.

> Leave it with me, "the king told her, I will see to it that no one touches him. Oh thank you my Lord she replied." "And I will take the responsibility if you are criticized for helping me like this."

> "Don't worry about that the King replied. If anyone objects bring them to me; I can assure you that he will not complain again." Then she said, "Please swear to me by God that you won't let anyone harm my son. I want no more bloodshed."

> "I vow by God he replied, "Not a hair of your son's head shall be disturbed. [II Samuel 14:8-11 LB]

Then of course the real motive of the plot is revealed. David is again the object of the plot to correct a grievance to which he has contributed substantially. This time he correctly surmises that Joab is behind the "widow story", in order to allow the banished Absalom to return. David relents, but only partially. He will allow Absalom to return, but then he will have nothing to do with him. Let's follow David's words that allow the return of Absalom.

"The King however gave orders that Absalom should not live in the palace. I don't want to see him the King said. "[II Samuel 14:24 GNB]

Michelangelo's David has much to admire from many different angles. So too does Biblical literature have much to admire from different angles. The beauty of Biblical stories is that they can often be infused with multiple meanings if one is willing to look. Sometimes though there are multiple meanings that may not only be at odds with other potential meanings, but also sometimes in extreme contrast. Taking this another step, sometimes the beauty of the Bible is the transparency that shows the flawed side of God's agents. . Take the story with the woman from Tekoa who Joab enlists to convince David to bring back Absolom to the country. Recall that he had fled after killing the man who raped his sister when David ignored the whole event. David had also declined Absolom 's hospitality along the way.

We are told that Absolom has fled in exile and fear, but that David very much wants him back, even though he has killed a potential heir to the throne. This is something that David would not do directly when he himself had a chance to be king sooner and with justification given both the wickedness of Saul and the subsequent anointing of David. Enter Joab who senses the distress of David and devises a plan to have Absolom return from exile. He enlists a wise woman from Tekoa to contrive a story that will tug on David's sense of justice. In this story the pretentious widow will utter some platitudes that are almost irresistible to David.

The temptation to preach on this platitude is nearly irresistible. The problem we precaution is to preach on some limited aspect while ignoring others. In the widow's challenge, depending on the version she recognizes that we all must die and that as such God does not respect anyone differently in that aspect. Then she implies that though we as humans cannot bring people back to life, as in perhaps some reference to the brother that Absolom killed, there are some things within our capacity as humans especially if we are king. To be blunt, David can return Absolom from exile. The King James Version and the NIV both note that God devises ways to bring back the banished. Other versions parallel this thought. Finally she applies flattery suggesting that because David is wise that he will figure out a way.

David may indeed have some discernment by seeing Joab as behind the ruse. His allowance of his exiled son to return home is conditional though. He will refuse to see him. For that matter so will Joab who orchestrated the whole matter. That is, until Absolom gets his attention by burning his fields. Finally he gets his appointment with the king. He immediately sets about getting his own coalition through the guise of delayed and unfulfilled justice. This eventuates in mutiny with the tables turned and David going into exile. Joab ultimately kills the man he worked to get back, the insurrections, Absolom.

What were the motives of the key players. Was Joab trying to contain an exiled threat by bringing him back where he could be observed? Was Absolom ever truly repentant or did he have ulterior motives from the beginning. Was David as wise as the Tekoa woman alluded, did he discern the risk, or was this just another example of his negligence as a parent where he does not extend any hand for forgiveness? Was the woman really wise or was she just platitudinous and invoking God's name and flattery? We get some strong clues in the outcome of the process but what is not told in the internal story actually tells the real story. None of the characters involved ever once calls upon God during the entire ordeal. Accordingly we must be cautious of assigning too much significance to an event even though platitudes and God's name are invoked. Indeed much harm has been done in the name of God.

But wait, it's true that the widow's visit and words were contrived, primarily to produce a sense of shame in David and an end result that would benefit Absolom and Joab's political desires. Nonetheless there is a very profound meaning in the statement that may in many ways apply to all of us.

Let's examine the widow's indirect criticism of David's continued banishment of Absolom: "God devises ways so that a banished person does not remain banished from him".

In other words, "release him, God would".

At face value her statement seems to indicate that Absolom's restoration from banishment is a unilateral act- God simply restores and so should David release and restore his son. And while it's true and profound that God desires and produces restoration, God would and could not do that unilaterally. It would be incomplete. There's more to restoration, it's at least a three act relationship endeavor, and at least two of the acts were missing in the Absolom restoration the widow and David are discussing.

Restoration from banishment, evil or to a favored position depends on repentance and forgiveness, both of which were missing in the Absolom and David transaction. While you can argue that David's agreement to restore Absolom implied forgiveness, David did not offer it, nor did Absolom ask for it. And neither did David suggest or ask for repentance as a condition to return to his favor.

What if questions of forgiveness and repentance had been raised and debated? Would the anger guilt and resentment that existed between David and Absolom have been mollified and reduced to a point that avoided the future disaster of Absolom's revolt, Israel's pain, and David's meltdown? The problems and issues of guilt, shame and

Dr. Stephen Harrison And Richard Huizinga

anger that existed between them were not confronted and were not subjected to the healing powers of repentance and forgiveness. The essential problems were ignored. No long term peace ensued for Israel, and the political solution to banishment relief bore no merit.

The widow was right, God restores. But she never relayed the total solution. And despite the Psalms he authored, David failed to see the solution from his own pen. (or,"he wrote about so often")

Absalom is indeed an enigma. On the one hand it is quite possible that his destiny is to be king-if he doesn't mess up. What happens though if his father the king and his brother mess up? What is admirable to a degree is that he takes care of business when his sister is raped and David does nothing. Also, admirable from a certain angle is his willingness to sit at the gate and mete out justice that people perceive they had not received. To be clear he is building a coalition, but why do people perceive the need for a different justice and therefore a different leader? Absalom cannot perform a revolt without other leaders including military. Who would these individuals likely be? The leading pool of candidates are those seeking more power, perhaps displaced individuals, but more likely younger individuals by ten to fifteen years than David's leaders. Joining Absalom is their best bet to hitch a ride to power.

Ultimately there must have been some rationalization though that justifies their actions. That justification may well be things we have referenced here and elsewhere, namely David not delivering justice. David becoming complacent. Absalom followers would have had some president in a king being removed that paved the way for David's rule. Why not a repeat performance? Their convictions may be strengthened more by each move David makes for a while, such as fleeing the imperial city at the mere mention of the coming of Absalom to take over. He leaves the harem behind knowing they will be despoiled as prophesied. He even revokes his pledge to Jonathan's offspring when a servant suggests that that offspring was part of the revolt-without bothering to check any of the details. This is the reactionary David at his worst.

When it is all said and done though, David goes to the extreme to not want Absalom executed despite his uprising. When that execution happens, David mourns to such a degree the he must be reprimanded by his own leadership in order to stop a mutiny among his own men because David was lamenting the loss of his enemy who was trying to kill him and usurp the throne. Why the deep lament? David, after all, had plenty of other heirs. He did not appear close to any of his other children including Absalom. Was it because he wanted to eventually reconcile and forgive? Yes forgiveness is part of the package. Just not what you would think-or hope. After all, when Absalom returns from exile, David won't even meet with him until Absalom himself takes dramatic actions. He even offers up his own life if he is found to be in the wrong. Absalom, like Jonathan, is willing to sacrifice himself for the cause. One consideration is that David actually greatly admired Absalom and his willingness to deliver justice where David had failed. He needed Absalom to teach him how to be a better person, a better family man, and deliverer of justice, etc. Yes to a degree Absalom had shown the value of forgiving debts when he sat at the gates that David never did. Or would. Ever.

Next we turn to one of the most poignant stories in the Bible. As you may recall, David has committed sin by sleeping with Bathsheba and then killing Bathsheba's husband Uriah when he refused to sleep with her so that the paternity of the baby from the union of David and Bathsheba could be attributed to Uriah. But alas, Uriah is too faithful, and will not have relationships with even his wife when the country is at risk and he is at war. Nathan proceeds to tell the story of the rich man who had a guest to entertain, but would not sacrifice any of his many sheep. Instead he took the one and only prize lamb of his poor neighbor. Nathan wishes to dramatize the connection of the family with the sheep portrayed so well in the ERV, "the poor man fed the lamb and the lamb grew up with the poor man and his children. She ate from the poor man's food and drank from his cup. The lamb slept on the poor man's chest. The lamb was like a daughter to the poor man". [II Samuel 12:3 ERV] A good shepherd like David is enraged and demands stiff penalties. [II Samuel 12:5-6 any version] David burned with anger against the man and said to Nathan, "as sure as the Lord lives, the man who did this must die! He must pay for the lamb four times over, because he did such a thing and had no pity." [II Samuel 12:5 NIV] What a shock to David when Nathan reveals that the story is about David. While on the one hand David is indeed humbled by the tone of that story and penitent, by the same token this is exactly the situation in which Samuel describes, in which the king will take the prize animals. (I Samuel 8: 10-18)

This event with Bathsheba leads to the perpetual threat of murder in David's household and indeed predates the Absalom/Amnon event. While David will acknowledge the event and confess the sin, the child product of the illicit affair must die. Perhaps God cannot stand to have an illegitimate son on the throne, conceived out of wedlock. Furthermore David's wives, according to the curse will be given to another man who will bed them in public. David naturally confessed. Who wouldn't? Nathan acknowledges that David will be forgiven and not die for his transgression. So far as God and Nathan are concerned though, the biggest transgression by David is the poor example that David sets for other nations. "But you have given great opportunity to the enemies of the Lord to despise and blaspheme him, so your child shall die." [II Samuel 12:14 LB] It looks like God cares about reputation as much and more than David does. It is as if God says, "Hey Pal it is one thing to damage your own reputation for which there must be consequences. On the other hand, if you damage mine, we are talking some serious consequences, including the deserved death that you mentioned in the Nathan parable. It is simply that the child will serve as the substitute for that deserved death. If you are a man after God's heart you must be an example to others, even those not in the same faith."

Why is the Nathan parable so more effective than the "widow parable". Is it because:

1. In the Nathan parable David is the one being forgiven and senses the urgency of the matter and the potential to avert death.
2. Following this concept of forgiveness, is it because when David is the one doing the forgiving that he really cannot completely forgive?
3. Is this part of the control factor that David likes to have that can be an incredible passive aggressive perspective by saying nothing?
4. Is it because he considers Nathan a spokesman for God, but not the widow?
5. Is it because the widow is a woman and Nathan a man?
6. Is it because David has already been pulled into the story of Nathan all the way preceding this and then made a wide open oath that openly condemned himself, as opposed to the widow's story where he catches on after making a partial oath of protection?

Whatever your perspective we are left with incomplete resolution in the Absalom/widow story.

David indeed has issues when it comes to reconciliation and forgiveness if he is the one that feels slighted. As such, it is difficult to feel that forgiveness is what God had in mind when he said that David was a man after God's own heart. The king appears willing to keep his oath, although avoid seeing Absalom after his return following the widow's story. But, Absalom appears desperate to see his father, King David. First, Absalom appeals to David's right hand man, Joab, to get an audience with the king. While Joab has indeed orchestrated Absalom's return, Joab will have nothing to do with him until Absalom sets fire to Joab's fields in order to get Joab's attention. Joab then reluctantly agrees to meet him and Absalom delivers his rehearsed speech. "I want you to arrange for me to see the King, and if I am guilty, then let him put me to death." [II Samuel 14:32 GNB] This is perhaps the original version of the psychological game "the prisoners dilemma." David may indeed have ignored Absalom because he did not follow that part of God's heart for forgiveness; instead, he may have had a fear of Absalom. Perhaps both David and Joab feared Absalom more when he was away and there was trouble he could stir up, but less when he was back. Otherwise, why would David not talk to Absalom after he returned? Perhaps the gut fear of power surge to Absalom if so there was a full recognition and reconciliation was on the back of David and Joab's minds. If so their intuition was correct. The thought process that they exercised though did not involve God in any apparent way, as there is absolutely no mention of God during that timeframe. Meanwhile, Absalom has nothing to lose since his life is already fading away. He appeals to David's conscience through Joab. He also knows full well that he will not be accused by David of committing murder, because people would see his actions as legitimate retribution for a serious family matter. Absalom is shrewd and uses that shrewdness that he has learned from his father David, to build a coalition that gives David much concern. Indeed, out of that gut fear, David flees Jerusalem and does not consult God. This is not the only time a gut fear reaction appears to be an opposition to the heart of God. David will then see shortly another component of David's prophecy fulfilled when he leaves several wives and concubines behind that Absalom takes advantage of.

There are other instances when it appears that David is forgiving, only to have his vengeful factor surface. One of the stories where there is a great gap between the event and resolution is that of Shimei. In II Samuel chapter 16, while David is fleeing from Absalom Shimei throws stones at the king and his officers and all of the entourage of mighty warriors. Then he shouts out, "Get out! Get out! Murderer! Criminal! You took Saul's kingdom, and now the Lord is punishing you for murdering so much of Saul's family. The Lord has given the kingdom to your son Absalom, and you are ruined, you murderer!" [II Samuel 16:7-8 GNB] David's seeming high road here is to leave the man alone, because perhaps God is telling the man to curse David. "My own son is trying to kill me; and this Benjaminite is merely cursing me. Let him alone, for no doubt the Lord is telling him to do it." [II Samuel 16:11 GNB] Note, with this line of thinking God puts words in Shimei's mouth that David correspondingly knows how to read the mind of God, which simply shows how displaced he is at the moment. David even adds a spin to the process that because of the cursing that maybe God would catch wind of his plight and intervene. "Perhaps the Lord told him the curse; so leave him alone and let him do it. Perhaps the Lord will notice my misery and give me some blessings to take the place of his curse." [II Samuel 16:11-12 GNB]. Later after David is reestablished as King of Israel he again forgives Shimei when his soldiers want to put him to death. [II Samuel 19]

All of this sounds like a great attitude until you get to the end of David's life. In First Kings Chapter 2, we have a completion of the story with his bitter vengeance. On his death bed David tells Solomon, "Do you remember Shimei the son of Gera the Benjaminite from Bahurim. He cursed me with a terrible curse as I was going down to Mahanaim, but when he came down to meet me at the Jordan River I promised I wouldn't kill him. But, that promise does not bind you! You are a wise man and you will know how to arrange a bloody death for him." [I Kings 2:8-9 LB] "Now do not consider him innocent. You are a man of wisdom; you will know what to do with him. Bring his gray head down to the grave in blood." Paybacks: as a human being you have to love David. This is not likely the heart that God is referring to. David has a similar chance at forgiveness to someone who simply denies him services and supplies that David and his men could use during their travels on the road as warriors. The individual is Nabal and he will deny David the request for desired resources. David is bent on retaliation for that denial. When he sets off to exact the vengeance he believes Nabal deserves, Nabal's wife Abigail gets wind of Nabal's error and sets out to correct it. Meanwhile, David has uttered a strong oath – one that he will not ultimately keep. Let's turn to the KJV so that we can grasp both the severity and its prudence. "And so more also do God unto the enemies of David, if I leave of all that pertain to him by the morning light any that pisseth against the wall." [I Samuel 25:22 KJV] David will be talked out of this episode of total annihilation by a woman, Abigail, who has deceived her husband, called him names and flattered David. We will have more to say on this issue later.

It is one thing to have common scoundrels' curse you or deny you services when David may not have the heart to forgive. But, what about someone who saved David's life arguably and tried to give him credit for a the key victory and even gave some key advice on several occasions that David did not heed, such as when he warned David not to do the senseless census that led to many deaths. Enter

Joab, David's main General. Joab has been David's right hand man and arguably done deeds that needed to be done and that David would not do. He also gave credit to David for victories that he could have claimed on his own. Let's look at chapter 12 of Second Samuel again. Basically this is the chapter where David is confronted about Bathsheba by Nathan. David seeks forgiveness, loses the baby, has relations with Bathsheba to console her, and procreate Solomon all in the same chapter. But, the chapter is not over. Rather, David is getting back on his feet and could use a good old fashion war victory or two. Joab is closing in on such a victory when he holds up the Army so that David can get credit. Joab sent messengers to David and said; "I have fought against Rabbah and have captured his water supply. Now bring the rest of the army together and attack Rabbah. Capture this city before I do, or else it will be called by my name." [II Samuel 12:27-28 ERV]

It was Joab who killed Abner who was in a plot to have Saul's heirs on the throne instead of David. Joab was also the one who killed Absalom when he arose in insurrection against his father. The death of Absalom will lead to great grief by David and a loss of perspective. It is Joab who will try to shed a favorable light on this whole episode. In fact, he notes that after David makes such a deal about all of the loss of Absalom that the soldiers in David's army are dejected and ready to abandon David because he has humiliated them in his persistent weeping and mourning over the loss of the enemy. Joab notes that unless David turns around his attitude, it will be the worst disaster of his life. What is Joab's reward for arguably saving the King's life at least once? He is demoted. The demotion seems to be because David has a relative who can provide him with a more complete opportunity to restore his entire throne. He does not mention the killing of Absalom at that time nor on his death bed, as he senses how politically compromising this would be. But, what does David do on his death bed? He condemns Joab to death. "There is something else. Do you remember what Joab did to me by killing the two commanders of Israel's Army, Abner son of Ner and Amasa son of Jether. You remember how he murdered at a time of peace in revenge for deaths they had caused in times of war. He killed innocent men. And now I bear the responsibility for what he did, and I suffer the consequences. You know what to do. You must not let him die a natural death." [I Kings 2:5-6 GNB] These are David's words to Solomon on his death bed. The mention of God's gift of wisdom to Solomon in the same sentence as his instructions to murder his longstanding General are more than a curious incident. Rather, their juxtaposition with the mention of Solomon's wisdom is a part of the cold hearted, calculated, shrewdness of David. They do not appear to be a part of the heart of God. Conspicuously absent is the mention to murder Joab for killing David's insurrectionist son Absalom. David has no doubt sensed that this would not be politically popular since the existing standard of death would have been done to any insurrectionist including family. David does not wish to be unpopular, even on his death bed. The fact that Solomon waits to take this process a step further and wait until he has a rebellious charge against Joab before killing him is simply a reflection of having learned shrewdness from the master of shrewd himself, David. We must not forget the role that Joab played in the murder of Uriah at the request of David. More on this later.

Joab was not the only one to have great retaliation against themselves from David as opposed to from God despite saving David's life. In fact, arguably Joab is able to live out a pretty full life even after his demotion for the family and political reasons. Imagine, though, that the King has fought and killed for you, bargained for your return after you were taken away, and then you lived a life of shame and watched your children brutally murdered due to one of David's arrangements. All of this actually occurred after such an individual had saved the King's life. This is the story of Michal. Arguably she suffered a fate much worse than death. Recall that Michal was considered enough as a prize, as the King's daughter, that David killed over two hundred men after King Saul thought he had set too high of a price for her dowry. This was even after Saul had reneged on his pledge to give one of his daughters to the man who killed Goliath. Michal shows her loyalty to the arrangement with David by placing David in a basket and lowering him to the ground from a window in order to save David's life when he is being pursued by King Saul. Imagine the headlines for David. "Pretender to the throne saved by woman by hiding him in a basket." Maybe this concept ultimately got to David.

After all, Michal will pay not once but twice for trying to control the exuberance and excesses of David. Let us review II Samuel Chapter 6. After a great victory David wishes to celebrate by bringing the Ark of the Lord to a new residence. When one of the bystanders tries to steady the ark, he is struck dead by God. This infuriates David, while at the same time causes great fear in him. Just prior to this David had been dancing and celebrating before the Lord with the victorious Israelites. After this he called a halt to the festivities and they left the ark rest where it was. Over time this place where the ark resides comes to be greatly blessed and David gets wind of this. David then decides he needs that ark and those blessings and sends his followers to go and retrieve it. After just six steps of movement the carriers decide they should stop and celebrate the fact that they haven't died apparently and make sacrifices to God. David decides to outdo them and once again dance before the Lord. Apparently he danced really hard. "David danced before the Lord with all his might and with wearing priest clothing." [II Samuel 7:14 LB]. Now we see David and all his libido playing one of his many roles, this time mimicking a priest. But, enter Michal watching from a window, perhaps the same window she lowered David from to save his life. While watching from the window she saw David leaping and dancing and had great contempt for him. Michal rebukes David who then goes into a defense of sorts with a story. "I was dancing before the Lord who chose me above your father and his family who appointed me as leader of Israel, the people of the Lord! So, I am willing to act like a fool in order to show my joy to the Lord. Yes, and I am willing to look even more foolish than this, but I will be respected by the girls of whom you spoke." [II Samuel 6:21-22 LB]. David struck some deep blows with the family reference and the added spin that he was dancing before the Lord. Yes he knew the young ladies were watching and he would do it again under the notion of being foolish for God, but he saves the last blow for Michal, perhaps out of kingly reciprocal courtesy, he lets God strike Michal barren for the rest of her life.

Let's examine closely what Michal said to him. "How glorious the King of Israel looked today. He exposed himself to the girls along the street like a common pervert!" [II Samuel 6:20 LB] At first glance this sounds like some harsh language from someone who is a bit jealous. A pervert? The Message has Michal compare him to a burlesque dancer. The ERV gets even more graphic. "…you took off your clothes in front of your servant girls. You were like a fool who takes off his clothes without shame." [II Samuel 6:20 ERV]. According to the Good News Bible, "David wearing only a linen cloth around his waist danced with all his might to honor the Lord." [II Samuel 6:14 GNB].

There doesn't seem to be much debate, but one way or the other David let it all hang out. In fact, the word used in the story from the New American Bible is with abandon. David's version is that he let it all hang out for the Lord. Michal's version is that under the pretense of celebration for God he let it all hang out for the young women. Michal will suffer twice for this implication. Long stretches pass before she is heard from, not just barren, but missing in action. Then her name is mentioned as having adopted five sons from her sister. [II Samuel Chapter 21]. David will allow these sons to be taken from her and brutally executed for sins that Michal's father, Saul did years ago. Pardon me, but do you think your worst enemy or even the Mafia could compose a scene to top this? This does not seem to be the heart of God. This rather is a cold heart of stone that is crushing and not one of any redeeming human traits let alone the heart of God.

CHAPTER 2 QUESTIONS

1. Why does David respond more favorably to a poor man's story about sheep than a poor widows lost son?
2. Why does David refuse to speak to Absalom upon his return from exile?
3. Was David worried that Joab knew too much after Joab had given him great victories, saved his life, etc.?
4. Does Michal appear to have been treated fairly by David after she saved his life?
5. Is David's penchant for vengeance longer than his penchant for forgiveness?

CHAPTER 3
MOTIVES AND MOTIVATION

- David and Goliath. . .no booty, no fight.
- Medically speaking how does Bathsheba get pregnant?
- What is the difference between the morning after verses the after mourning?
- Abigail – the first attractive wife of another that David takes.
- The slingshot quote. . .where beauty and flattery led to breaking an oath.
- How to leave your wives behind and then ignore them upon return.
- David benefits from other's intimacy.
- Take my woman that I myself have taken and I will curse you. (Abner)
- What price do you pay for killing David's enemies?
- David loses his mojo?
- What the queen knew and what the most beautiful woman meant to a failing king and a potential contender for the throne.

When Michelangelo sculpted David in the nude, he did not appear to making any sexual statements. However, it is impossible to approach David without an understanding of the role of sex and sexism in his life. This statement is not intended to sound judgmental or anachronistic. It is also said, though, in order to not cover up what is already there. For example, most people familiar with the story of Bathsheba feel like we can forgive David just like God and Nathan for this one time indiscretion for which he repented. We may even appreciate the rich fictional story God gives the prophet Nathan to call attention to David's blunder. You have to love a God who uses David's own shepherd background to dramatize the situation. Nathan knew that David was fully aware of the value of a single sheep, especially to a poor family. David had after all bragged in public to what lengths he would go to salvage one sheep in his speech before fighting Goliath. Indeed, the saga of David is framed with conquest that involves women as much as any battlefront, although, it may not be obvious at first glance. We may have to remove the bias and our blinders to see this. Recall the story of Goliath, which is David's meteoric rise to fame. No doubt what comes to mind is an innocent, inexperienced, shepherd boy who takes on and defeats the giant who taunted Israel. This victory stimulates Israel to have a great rout over the Philistines. But, let us recall the background. David is already an experienced and accomplished fighter we are told in the preceding chapter. According to the GNB David is a good soldier and the Lord is with him. According to the NIV he is a brave man and warrior. According to the ERV he is a brave man and fights well. According to the KJV he is a mighty valiant man and man of war. [1 Samuel 16:18] Also, not so obvious is that David does not appear to be so anxious to fight Goliath, simply because he is taunting Israel and their God. He may indeed not be afraid of Goliath's stature, because he knows the power of the slingshot as described in Malcolm Gladwell's book, "David and Goliath". However, he does not fight Goliath until he verifies that there is a reward. What exactly is the reward that motivates him? Fame? Arguably, he already had that from the previous chapter. The specified reward for defeating Goliath includes money, some tax free status for family and one of the King's daughters. Perhaps this latter, seemingly sexist measure, was a reasonable ploy to keep a hero in the family and be less of threat to the throne. We will gloss over the fact that Saul's daughter has no say in the matter.

Our focus here is what motivates David. That motivation appears to be hormones and power. Would tax free status be that motivating for a poor shepherd boy who did not own much to begin with? Along those lines, what would a poor shepherd boy need money for since he had the only food, land and housing that he could appreciate. Ah, but there was a woman involved and a young man. The young man was already proven in battle, but he had no booty to show for it. Arguably the sex drive meant more to him than the power drive initially, though, he is able to win a king's daughter by this motivation when he kills two hundred Philistines. When he is denied one king's daughter and then has a chance for another he proves he has no need for a dowry or money. He cannot yet fully appreciate the power of a king to dispose of women at his discretion. Again, I do not wish to judge any character by taking actions out of time and context. That would be anachronistic moralism. It would not be proper to focus on either the class implications of David's ordeal or the sexism. That would detract us from David's motivation of hormonal opportunity.

Let us turn to one of David's most famous hormone encounters. It would not be an anachronism though to reflect on Bathsheba's role and options available, even for women in her time. First of all, she had to know that she was potentially visible to the king from his vantage point of the elevated palace. We are told that she was bathing as part of her purification following her period. This raises a series of implications and questions. First, she is exposed and we are told that she is stunningly beautiful. We should not think of her as naive. She was aware of her cycle and arguably knew what part of her cycle she could get pregnant. Arguably, David observed the woman and knew it was the time of purification right after her period. He too may have had a reasonable notion that a one night stand would not lead to pregnancy. Of course, Bathsheba does take up the invitation to go to the King. She does not appear to show any resistance or reluctance, nor do there appear to be any threats to her if she does not go. Nor does there appear to be any mention on her part that she is a married woman, married no less than one of David's top generals by the name of Uriah.

We know of course the outcome of what happens next. There is intimacy between David and Bathsheba. She returns to her own home only to send word shortly that she is pregnant. Keep in mind that medically speaking that the rights of purification could not possibly have lasted long enough to overlap with the mid-cycle timing for pregnancy. This leaves us with a number of options since she did indeed get pregnant.

1. This affair was more than a one night stand. David may have pleasured himself with intimacy on several occasions over a seven to ten day stretch.
2. Bathsheba was wrong about her cycle. Perhaps she had some spotting that she mistook for a period and so was vulnerable still in a one night stand.
3. She extended the rights of purification to give anyone who gave the appearance they might be observing that she was not at risk for becoming pregnant in that time of her cycle.
4. She had only a one night stand with David and was not in a vulnerable time with her cycle. However, she had a sexual encounter with someone else after the David encounter and that child was not David's. Perhaps this is why God said that the baby must die.
5. There was an immaculate conception. We can probably rule this out because there was a tragic death of the baby, but we

should not rule out God using an immaculate conception only to sacrifice that conception for a greater cause. If David is used as a prototype for The New Testament in Jesus then this version would have more credence than a superficial examination would give it.

Most people will probably select the first choice, though, there is no foolproof evidence for this, just as there is no evidence against any of the other choices. I am not proposing one theory over another, other than to note that whatever one is chosen must square both medically and with the story. What is certain is that your choice will reflect your bias more than it reflects facts.

Suffice to say, that Bathsheba knew she could get pregnant in a brief encounter with the King and counted on the King to provide a solution. This was another version of the prisoner's dilemma. Bathsheba knows that her options are limited. She likely surmises that the gravest consequences would be if her husband Uriah finds out that she is pregnant at all. She might face the consequences of no support or even death. In that scenario she would not inform Uriah who the father was. In related manner, in scenario two, she reveals that David the King is the father. In that situation she might have the edge that she would not die and might even be shipped off to live with the King. Or, if she did not go to live with the King then perhaps her baby would become a rare, medically and historically speaking, bastard king, after serving a role as a prince. She chooses instead to leave the choice to David, likely sensing that the best chance for she and the baby are to be under the care of the King. She had to sense that would be the end of life with Uriah as she knew it, one way or the other. She may have sensed that it was the end of life as Uriah knew, in the literal sense. What she could not conceive was that her baby would die.

We will discuss in another section various reasons why God may have been displeased for what David did. However, we do not have strong suggestion that God is displeased with Bathsheba, unless of course, you count the baby dying as a sign of displeasure. In Second Samuel, Chapter 11 we are told that the Lord was very displeased with what David had done. The immediate action antecedent is bringing Bathsheba to live with him. In fact, we are given the impression that David knew exactly when the wife of Uriah was complete with her mourning. The event before that was having Uriah killed. Before that there was the deed of sleeping with Bathsheba. Before that it was lusting after and coveting another man's wife. This was a combination of the Ten Commandments violation along with The New Testament admonition by Jesus that anyone who looks with lust at a woman has already committed adultery with her in his heart. More on this in another section.

Before departing this segment we might distinguish the difference between the morning after and the after mourning. Bathsheba is ready to have David deal with the morning after, which is the awareness of responsibility. She is also ready for David to take her into his house after mourning for her husband. In fact, she appears very ready. David meanwhile, was not prepared to deal with the morning after. His aides however were not prepared to deal with the after mourning. David did his mourning and fasting for the baby while it lived, but immediately following the baby's death he ended his fast and got on with life, which his aids did not understand. "While the child was alive he said, "I fasted and wept thinking God might have mercy on me and the child would live. Now that he is dead, why fast? Can I bring him back now? I can go to him, but he can't come to me." [II Samuel 12:22-23 MSG] Is David suggesting that if he doesn't get some nourishment and get on with the rest of life, that he too will be dead? Or is this a portion of the heart of God which appreciates the now and does not dwell in the past.

Bathsheba is not the first woman that David has that was the wife of another. We have mentioned the story elsewhere about Abigail who deceived her husband after he had refused to give David provisions. Sensing total annihilation for her people, Abigail comes to the rescue with food and flattery. There will be no intimacy yet until the rapid fall and demise of her husband. Her first flattery speech to David is one that she ends by saying that, "when he Lord has blessed you sir, please do not forget me." [I Samuel 25:31 Good News Bible] All this occurs after she has cursed her husband who is alive and deceived him, called him names, etc. Keep in mind David breaks an oath for this woman. After all who could resist a woman who says the following, "forgive my presumption! But God is at work in my master developing a rule solid and dependable. My master fights God's battles! As long as you live no evil will stick to you. If anyone stands in your way, if any one tries to get out of his way, know this: your God honored life is tightly bound in the bundle of God-protected life; but the lives of your enemies will be hurled aside as a stone is thrown from a sling". [I Samuel: 25:28-29 MSG] Yes, Abigail seems to know fortune and opportunity. David also knows opportunity and immediately on the death of Abigail's husband he asked her to be his wife. Abigail already has five ladies in waiting to accompany her for this anticipated event. In the Message she invokes the ultimate metaphor for David in the slingshot.

Why of course should David be the only one of his time to have his way with women? We have already detailed Amnon and the rape of his sister Tamar and how that set up the whole Absalom event. Ultimately Absalom will sleep with ten of David's wives/concubines after David flees for his life in fear. The scriptures tell us that David left behind ten concubines/wives to care for the palace. Come on

David, who are kidding here? You know Nathan's prophecy about another man sleeping with your wives. You know the revenge mode. You know the strongest showing a new king can make is to sleep with the deposed King's wives/concubines. We recall God's words to David, "I saved you from Saul, I let you take his family and his wives and I made you King of Israel and Judah." [ERV Second Samuel 12:7] All this goes down just as one might predict. What is not so obvious is that when David comes back to the kingly city, is that he will have nothing to do with these women that he left behind as booty for Absalom. That was not the first time protecting the women in his life did not appear to have high priority. Earlier while he was off fighting battles for the Philistine, his own camp is plundered. Men have lost their entire families and David has lost two wives in the ordeal. He seems rather casual about this until mention is made of talk about his men stoning David to death. This is the wakeup call he apparently needed to call upon the Lord. So here we have the mighty warrior with no rescue plan for the men's families who fought for him and risked their lives or even two of his own wives, until he has a death threat. This is the disposable aspect of David. The man who has killed with a single stone knows that certainly a collective body of man can indeed stone him to death. [I Samuel 30:1-6] We have seen several incidences like this where David has no problem getting women, but is less certain what to do with them when under pressure. Next, we will turn our attention to an episode where David is the beneficiary of someone else having intimacy, before finally looking at how his not having relations with a beautiful young women is linked to a coup against him and his death.

First, we will detail how David appears to be the beneficiary of someone else having intimate relations with the enemy. In this situation we have concubines who belong to Saul and then arguably Saul's son, Ish-Bosheth, who is the King by inheritance over Israel.

The culmination will occur when David has an opportunity to also have intimacy with someone who has been in a relationship with the enemy, someone he desperately wants, someone whom he could have legitimate relations with and then ultimately refuses to have serious relationships with her, much to the lady's disappointment. Before it is all said and done, two of the key players will be dead over the events.

Let's look at the details. In Second Samuel Chapter 3, Abner sleeps with one of Saul's concubines after Saul fell on his own sword and died. Saul's son Ish-Bosheth is reigning king who has inherited the rights to these concubines. He calls General Abner out on this, but Abner will not be shamed over this. "Am I a Judean dog to be kicked around like this he shouted. After all I have done for your father by not betraying you to David is this my reward-that you find fault with me about some woman? May God curse me if I don't do everything to take away the entire kingdom from you, all the way from Dan to Beersheba, and give it to David, just as the Lord predicted." [II Samuel 3:8-10 LB] After this speech King Ish-Bosheth was speechless himself.

While hormones or passion may be a great motivator, apparently its absence or the threat of its removal is even greater. After all, obviously Abner knew about the pledge from God to give the kingdom to David. While he obviously senses some power to expedite that, he has done nothing about it until the reigning king chastises him for having illicit relations. So, the immediate next move of Abner is to send a team to negotiate with David to give him the entire kingdom of Israel. Now, keep in mind that Abner had just insulted David's kingdom of Judah when he referred to being treated like a Judean dog. David doesn't appear to be too upset about the remark. However, before he will negotiate to receive a larger kingdom being handed to him by the key enemy general, David wants a woman from the other side. To be sure it is his original wife Michal, but considering how he will treat her after he has her back, one must wonder what his intentions were. Again, was this a power show similar to the modern mafia?

Before it is all over, the king being displaced, Ish-Bosheth, is going to arrange for his kingdom to be given away, give up his territorial rights over his concubine, and arrange for a man in his country to give away his wife to the enemy. What will be the fruits of his efforts? He will be murdered. But first, the man who stole the King's concubine must be punished-not by either king or for stealing the concubine. David's lead general, Joab will kill Abner as part of a payback because Abner killed Joab's brother, after Abner issued fair warning. Two brothers are appointed by King Ish-Bosheth to replace Abner. How do they reward the king? The brothers kill the king and bring his head to David as a symbol of their loyalty and to show David that he has nothing to fear. What then becomes their subsequent reward? They are killed by David's men at his request. What about the woman David wanted so badly that he couldn't take a free kingdom until she was part of the deal? That woman was his original wife Michal. We never had any evidence that he had relationships with her again for the rest of her life.

It is not clear how much of this amazing drama was for appearance, but it is very clear that not once does David call on God for direction during this entire stretch. He does not thank God for restoring his kingdom nor for returning his wife who had saved his life. To be sure, he does fast until sundown over Abner's death, which may have been for the appearance of uniting the kingdom, for which a fair portion has just been granted to him through Abner's work. There is no mention of prayer and fasting during this stretch, which so many references in the Bible pair up naturally. The only mention of God in these two chapters is when David uses God to swear by.

David answered them, "I will make a vow by the living Lord who has saved me from all dangers! The messenger who came to me Ziklag and told me of Saul's death thought he was bringing good news. I seized him and had him put to death. That was the reward I gave him for his good news! How much worse it will be for evil men who murder an innocent man asleep in his own house! I will now take revenge on you for murdering him and will wipe you off the face of the earth!" [II Samuel 4:9-11 GNB] David uses the swearing to justify killing people who once again, just like the news they brought him about Saul's death and thought they were doing him a favor, only to be rewarded by their own deaths. During this swearing phase David does appear to be attempting to give God credit for rescuing him from his enemies, but clearly Abner and Ish-Bosheth have been his enemies. Perhaps David perceived he did not need God for this little venture, as long as everything turned out fine. David will though, invoke God's name in order to justify some killing. David will have his ups and downs from here on until his final days, but hormonal passion will continue to play a major role throughout his life, even when he doesn't have it.

The stories of Michal, Joab, Shimei, and others are part of David's use of debt as a tool. This debt as tool is another useful metaphor to understand David. Ultimately David does not like to have a sense that he owes anyone anything, as this would imply a certain sense of ownership by the other party over David. The last thing that a self-made man would wish to have happen in his time would be to be dependent on a woman. In a sense this is what happened when his wife Michal, Saul's daughter saved his life by letting him out a basket from the window. She also perhaps saved him from embarrassment when she rebukes him in the story of David dancing before the arc of the Lord. David cannot be party to this type of dependence, as we have noted elsewhere the price that Michal pays for this ultimately, as one of an extreme nature, in which she is on the one hand barren and then subsequently has her adopted children brutally executed for the sins of her father. One therefore might ponder if this fate were worse than the men we shall highlight next.

The first individual we have mentioned elsewhere is Joab, David's key general. Ostensibly Joab is put to death by Solomon after David dies, at David's direction/recommendation. The reasons that he gives are somewhat trumped up and one must wonder what the real motives were that he put this off for many years in order to have somebody else deal with the process. After all, we must recall that Joab gave David credit for key victories in the battle at the last minute when David did essentially nothing and was furthermore able to take care of several of David's key enemies including David's insurrectionist son Absalom, as well as others. Is it possible in this situation that David simply did not wish to be beholden to anyone who had protected him to that degree or had a reputation that others knew about, in terms of who the real fighter was in certain key battles? In the long run Joab's execution appears to be a well orchestrated measure by David that was coolly calculated for a number of years in order to avoid political turmoil for the good that Joab accomplished. Absalom is arguably another person that must die because of a debt David owes him. After all Absalom acted when his sister was violated by another family member when David failed to take action. This is ultimately why he must die even if David did not calculate his death. Even if David mourns Absalom's death it is still an inevitability.

Perhaps the most unusual consideration of death, in order to avoid owing someone, was that of Uriah. On the surface Uriah had to die in order for David to have some type of access to Bathsheba. The proximate cause was the fact that Uriah would not sleep with Bathsheba in order to have any claim to the baby fathered by David.

Perhaps the ultimate cause though was beyond David having unrestricted access to Bathsheba. It is conceivable after all that Uriah would have forgiven David for this great offense as we mentioned in other sections. However, in so doing, David would have had a tremendous debt owed to Uriah. Ultimately this was not something David could live with. Given that legacy is a larger driving power for David than even the women in his life, how much more of a loss for Uriah is his death when we consider this perspective.

There are minor players who seem to pay a substantial cost, namely death, for having done some of David's bidding. To a lesser degree there are more minor players who have to die for their roles in David owing them. For example, all of the messengers involved in reporting the deaths of two of his enemy kings are subsequently put to death by David. The question in these situations are, did they die for killing the enemy, or for killing God's anointed or for lying. Or, did they simply know too much information that needed to be suppressed that David could not live with having someone knowing that information. Or, once again, was it a situation where he did not want to owe anyone anything because he could not stand that type of imbalance. In summary David does not know how to pay back the most innocent of messengers to the most loyal of his generals and to a wife who saved his life.

Earlier we mentioned how not having intimacy may have led to a coup for his kingdom and been a sign that his death was imminent. On the one hand, we do get some sense that David was starting to wear out [Second Samuel 21] where David was fatigued and leading his soldiers into battle. Indeed, all good things must come to an end in the ageing cycle and David is no exception. We will usher in this final phase of David's life with only one and half chapters left in his life. "In his old age King David was confined to his bed; but no matter how many blankets were heaped on him, he was always cold". [I Kings 1:1 Living Bible] As a physician of thirty years experience, it is a natural phenomenon to speculate what this condition was. With low energy and feeling cold, hypothyroidism is the first condition that comes to mind. To a lesser degree this could represent adrenal insufficiency, much like President John F. Kennedy. Further down the list might be an immune deficiency or autoimmune conditions. It is even possible that the plague mentioned in the preceding chapter has imposed these symptoms on David. It is also quite possible that testosterone deficiency is one candidate. It appears indeed that David's aids thoughts testosterone deficiency was worth trying to treat and sought the most beautiful woman in all the land. "A cure for this, his aids told him, is to find a young virgin to be your concubine and nurse. She will lie in your arms and keep you warm." [I Kings 1:2 LB] So they searched the land until they found the most beautiful girl and then connected her with David. Their diagnosis may have been correct, but their treatment did not produce the desired effect. She apparently kept him warm, but had no sexual relations with him. [I Kings 1:4] The Message often uses frank and graphic language and symbolism. Let's pick up in chapter one of First Kings. . . So his servants said to him, "we are going to get a young woman for our master, soon to be at his side and look after him; she will get in bed with you and arouse our master the King". So they searched the country of Israel for the most ravishing girl they could find; they found Abishag the Shunammite and brought her to the king. The girl was stunningly beautiful; she stayed at his side and looked after the King, but the King did not have sex with her [I Kings 1:1-4 The MSG] The intent here by the aides seemed fairly clear here-get an attractive young female to arouse the King, have sex and get some life in him. It just didn't work and not necessarily because David didn't want to go along with it. He seems willing enough to have her be there, but just not up to consummation. The sling shot is flaccid and has lost its potency.

No doubt, this failure to consummate message spread through the social media rapidly. The very next verse begins with "about this time. . ." The explanation following is that David's own son, Adonijah decided to crown himself king and makes some elaborate arrangements to that end. We don't think it is coincidental that after David's lack of intimacy that someone close to him usurps the throne. After all, if the King is no longer virile how is he going to put up any resistance to anyone trying to take the throne? In fact, David is not so much resisting a young woman as he is unable in Adonijah's eyes. So too does Adonijah sense that David cannot resist against a takeover. David has indeed lost the mojo that governed his life from the time of Goliath to his death.

ADDENDUM: As we note elsewhere David was attracted to beautiful women, as well as women of power. Who was the most powerful woman in his life?

While some versions tend to soften the interaction between Abishag and King David others will be quite clear what the intent seems to have been. What may not have been so clear is that she was also recognized as a woman of power besides her great beauty. There are hints of this in I Kings Chapter 1 when both Bathsheba and Nathan the prophet come and bow before her. Granted, they are actually bowing before King David, but Abishag is very clearly in the presence right next to the King and so affectively they are bowing before her. Notably though the power effect comes out in the next chapter in which Adonijah who had been trying to pull a coup for the kingship, now requests to marry Abishag. Interestingly he makes that request through Bathsheba and appeals to her to go before the new King Solomon for his request in marriage. Even more interesting, Bathsheba agrees to do this, though, one wonders what her motives and knowledge actually was. Upon hearing that his mother wished to see him, Solomon pulled out a throne for Bathsheba and had her sit on it while she made her request. He agreed in advance to supply whatever she asked for. However, when she made her blunt request for Adonijah to be able to wed Abishag this was flat out recognized by Solomon as an attempt to have the Kingdom given to Adonijah and said as much. This again goes back to the theory of the way to show officially that a king has been conquered is to sleep with his wives or concubines. While this was recognized by Solomon who then quickly had Adonijah killed over this event, there is a fair chance Bathsheba knew all along that the outcome would be when Adonijah made this request. This seems to be indirect evidence of her ability to be cunning and shrewd to the very end. As powerful as Bathsheba was, verse for verse, an argument can be made that Abishag is the most powerful woman in the Bible. She signifies the end of life for one king and is cause for death for a pretender to the throne all in a few verses.

As powerful as Abishag appears to be verse for verse, she is overshadowed by the totality of power displayed by Bathsheba. In today's culture we may struggle more than a little with the role that Bathsheba had. Just as she was not naïve, so too we would do well to not be naïve about her motives. It is so tempting to construct a scenario where she is the nearly innocent female who is simply fulfilling the female role predicted by Samuel. She is at the mercy of a king who sees it as his right to take advantage of her in any way he can. You can't stop prophecy or hormones for that matter. That is tidy and convenient, but perhaps not the complete story.

Elsewhere we mention how she may well have been more calculating and aware than meets the eye. Realistically there is a fair chance that she knew David well ahead of the affair. After all, her husband,

Uriah was a major general in David's army. There was likely some shared social circle status. As such, there is more than a fair chance that she knew David's interest and habits. We know his interest in women. She knew his habit of looking around, where he walked when he could not sleep, what he would be capable of seeing when he was walking, and what he was capable of doing when he was meandering.

She shared much in common with Abigail. Besides being married to a man of power, she attempts to portray herself in a favorable light to catch David's eye. In Abigail's situation it was daytime with a seeming self preservation motive to save her people. With Bathsheba it is a nighttime situation. How does David even see her? Unless, of course, she has provided the light to be seen. David may have peered over the balcony to see her but she has peered into his mind. David may have provided the hormonal spark, but she may well have stoked it into a fire. Both she and Abigail appear more than ready to join David's retinue after their husbands are disposed of by David.

CHAPTER 3 QUESTIONS

1. What really motivates David to fight Goliath?
2. To what degree did Bathsheba calculate her adventure with David?
3. How did David benefit from others having salacious encounters?
4. What happens when the most beautiful women in the land is unable to stimulate the aging king?
5. Under the circumstances, how is an argument made for Abishag being the most powerful female in the Bible, verse for verse?

CHAPTER 4
AUTHORITY AND
OVERLOOKED ENTITIES

- David . . . I may not be a good judge like Samuel so I will let God do the judging.
- Humility, accepting the smallest of roles.
- The giant . . . I know a big bad one when I see one.
- I will use my own tools if you please.
- "The thing" The Bathsheba affair and Ten Commandments
- God's reputation: you can destroy your own, but don't mess with God's.
- Hey, if you are going to do some extreme things at least be resilient.
- Senseless census . . . what happens when a man on the run stops running.
- How much reassurance does a man who has it all need?

One should not come away from this treatise feeling that hormones were the only motivating factor for David, or even necessarily the most important. There is a difference between saying that his life was framed by hormones and that you cannot understand David without looking closely at this aspect. It is also important to realize there are other key aspects that contribute to our image of David.

We do not set out to strip David down to a few traits and say we have uncovered the real man, anymore than Michelangelo sculpted David so that only one image would predominate. Rather, reading through David is a constant search for what his heart truly is, since he is a man after God's own heart. In order to have a more complete search for that heart of God, let us return to some of the themes we may have touched on and others that we have overlooked, while at the same time looking from different angles at some events we have already discussed.

In order to understand David, it is also important to realize the role that authority played in his life. David seems to have a high respect for authority, that is until he gets it himself. We have already mentioned how David's spared Saul on at least two occasions, out of respect of the authority that God had given to Saul. David does not see it as his duty to judge Saul or judge God, even when Saul has some very obvious questionable behaviors and traits that ran counter to any decency on heaven or earth. Even when Saul is trying to kill David and David recognized that he himself is God's next in line, he will not go against Saul's divine right to rule. Perhaps this is a glimpse into the heart of David that is what God sees: David does not judge people, especially people of authority, he will let God do that in his own time.

David begins his life by accepting the authority of the system that begins with honoring his parents. He performs the tasks that he is given by his father that include going to great lengths to protect that with which he is entrusted with, such as even the sheep who have been attacked by wild animals. Maybe this is another clue to David's heart. He trusts the system to the extent that the smallest details matter for him. Everything is part of the system and no part is too small to be let out of the system. By the same token David is sometimes seen as someone who stood up against family when they challenged his presence, such as on the battle field of Goliath where he extends his fame and fortune. Looking only at one rebuff by his oldest brother, is hardly enough evidence to build an entire picture of how David viewed his family or vice versa. From the perspective of the older brother Eliab at the battlefront, he is right to question David's motive at being at the battlefront. [I Samuel 17:28] Meanwhile, not much is made of the fact that later on David moved his parents when he perceived they were in trouble [I Samuel 22] In addition, all his brothers rally around him when they perceive he is in trouble. [I Samuel 22] Of course David went to the battlefront because he was instructed to do so by his father. As such, he was only doing his duty. That duty we have already been told included earlier active military duty where he had already accomplished significant military feats. It would be very difficult for most people to recognize a humble role of delivery boy if they sensed they were more capable of greater things. Perhaps this is what was meant by God's heart that he saw reflected in David: humility. Perhaps it was better acceptance of all the roles in one's life, noting that none were too small, if one accepts each moment as an opportunity to fulfill that role.

David of course sees a greater role on the battlefield than the delivery boy. He is willing to challenge authority when it does not align with the God of his understanding. Goliath has supplied literally a giant challenge to God's authority. David wants to know where Goliath gets his authority to defy the armies of the living God. He knows that such authority is not rewarded by stature. Perhaps this is another reflection of the heart of God: the ability to recognize what is not emanating from God or otherwise known as discernment. Coupled with this is another contender for the heart of God trait: The ability to see a larger, more important goal that supercedes the original goal. Of course, one has to have a flexibility and adaptability to make that quick adjustment to accomplish the larger goal. Perhaps what might be seen as only impulsivity or as reward seeking, as discussed further, is actually related to the heart of God concept. David indeed invokes God's authority to fight Goliath. This is one of clear times that he will show precedence for following God's authority over man's (his brother or King's authority). Saul has after all challenged the boy as inexperienced and a great underdog against Goliath. Nonetheless, if David sees it as his duty to fight the giant, Saul insists that David wear his armor. David obliges the King, but ultimately realizes that somebody else's clothes are not something he can step into. No, he will fight Goliath with the tools he had been given in life and mastered. Perhaps this is another of the heart of God concepts in that David recognizes that if he is going to fight big battles that he needs to do it with the tools he has been blessed with and not someone else's.

Once David is in a position of authority, though, he appears to lose sight of how that authority lies with the ultimate authority. There are certain areas time and again where the perspective of authority is lost. The classic example is of course with Bathsheba. David understands his kingly role as an opportunity to do as he pleases to a fair degree with his hormones. He conveniently sets aside God's Ten Commandments where there is clear recommendation. Obviously, David has broken the commandment against adultery. Obviously, he has broken the Commandment against murder during the ordeal. What is not so obvious is that he has broken the commandment against coveting anything that is his neighbors. It is not too much of a stress to say that he is born false witness against Uriah. Clearly, he has not honored his parents with this action.

Bathsheba is referred to as the wife of Uriah by several versions, including not just the King James version and the NIV, but also the Message, long after she comes to live with David. In fact, even after she weds David she is referred to as to the wife of Uriah in these versions and others until after the birth of the baby fathered by David and that baby's subsequent death. We believe these references are to highlight the fact that David has no rights to Bathsheba until the death of the baby fathered by David, because there could have been a claim even in death about a connection with Uriah for that baby. Let us turn to the conclusion of the adultery chapter where we read, "When Uriah's wife heard that her husband was dead, she mourned for him. After the time of mourning was over, David had her brought to his house and she became his wife and bore him a son. "But the thing David had done displeased the Lord." [II Samuel 11:26-27 NIV] The question here is, what is "the thing?" Let's look at the possibilities.

1. The adultery itself, this seems to be the most obvious answer and maybe the best if one is looking for only one answer. But, this treatise is about possibilities and not one answer only. The medical field is filled with many situations, in which the so called most obvious answer is the only one considered, only to prove erroneous often way down the road.

2. Killing Uriah, again another obvious choice and an infraction of the Ten Commandments.

3. Trying to induce Uriah to sleep with his wife. In this sense David goes to great lengths to try and cover up the likelihood that Bathsheba's baby is Uriah's. David even gets Uriah drunk to convince him to have relations Bathsheba. In so doing, he is attempting to get Uriah to dishonor his duty to his king, country and ultimately God. In fact, Uriah even mentions that the whole country of Israel and Judah are in tents along with the Ark of God. Under no circumstances will he violate that loyalty.

4. Weakening Uriah's legacy. Arguably the collusion that David brings about involving high up officials, in order to bring down Uriah, is conspiracy that would be construed as bearing false witness to Uriah's reputation.

5. Lusting. This is arguably the primordial event in the story. It is violating the covenant against coveting. It all began with taking that walk at night and looking.

6. Trusting God. As primordial as the above may be, we must ask ourselves why David could not sleep at night, which explains why he was up to begin with. Arguably it was because he had not entrusted all his concerns to God. He was tossing and turning because there were issues he had not turned appropriate to God. He had placed something in front of his relationship with God, which his consistent with a violation of the first two commandments.

7. It doesn't take too much to see that David is stealing something here, but what exactly is he stealing? Besides the obvious David is stealing Uriah's reputation and legacy. In a sense, the baby that Uriah did not conceive is still his. There is no chance to have a name sake otherwise that we are told.

8. Forgiveness. Uriah has no chance to exercise forgiveness to either Bathsheba or David. It is a bit presumptuous to think he would not have been willing to forgive, had it all been laid out on the line.

9. Timing. David appears to waste no time in bringing Bathsheba to live with him as his wife after the mourning period was over. This is the statement that immediately precedes the statement about "the thing." Perhaps the thing is that David did not show enough respect for the legitimate grief that people have over loss.

10. Paternity. Perhaps God is upset first that David has tried to pass on paternity appearances with a child to Uriah, but

later as though they were a natural sequence with an early birth not suggesting any illicit affair. Again the Bathsheba affair appears to be a risk analysis. If Uriah is killed quickly followed by short mourning, it is plausible that people will buy the notion that the child would be considered a product of a legitimate marriage. Some people know the truth, God knows and he will not have an illegitimate son sit on the throne at this time.

11. Reputation: God's, not David, as we see in II Samuel 12:14 that God appears disturbed about his reputation to other countries given David is his representation and has committed this great sin with Bathsheba.

The following drawn straight from the David and Bathsheba chapter is meant to serve as teaser and thought provoking process. Please reflect on what individual the following traits represent.

1. He was totally innocent.
2. A powerful king sought his death.
3. He resisted temptation even in challenging circumstances.
4. He was spied upon within his own circle.
5. He was betrayed and abandoned by those closest to him.
6. He was vilified
7. He was a servant who suffered.
8. He died an ignominious death.

Please see the addendum for the expansion of this topic.

After "the thing" we see that there is a wedding between David and Bathsheba, she comes to live with him, the baby is born, and the baby dies. After the death of this child David comforts Bathsheba in what may be arguably one of the most peculiar things to do when a woman has lost her child. On the one hand David soothes himself by having sex. This produces Solomon, which satisfies his "forever" need. On the other hand, he is able even under these circumstances to soothe his wife. Perhaps this is a part of the heart of God, that David can comfort those who are suffering no matter how great the suffering, and even if they contributed to their own calamity. Is this not exactly the situation when David calms Saul's tormented soul, even with the risk of spears coming at his head? David also has the ability to land on his feet after he has been confronted by authority that he recognizes and respects. This is indeed what happens after he is confronted by Nathan after the Bathsheba incident. When he recognizes God, whether directly or went through his agents, David may rebound incredibly. Perhaps this is what God meant by a man after his heart: resiliency. Anyone can get down, but it takes a real heart of God to rebound. This is indeed true resiliency and provide hope to those who otherwise do not see hope.

David's ability to rebound quickly is a trait he will need all through his career. Towards the end of his life, even after he has achieved great success, he will still fall prey to measures that most do not consider to be a reflection of God's heart. Let's take a look at the senseless census. This census is a bit hard to understand as to its origin. In II Samuel 24 we see that God was angry with Israel; so for some reason provokes David to take a census. The Message appears to put the most favorable spin on this as a test from God." Once again God's anger blazed out against Israel. He tested David by telling him, "go and take a census of Israel and Judah." [II Samuel 24:1 MSG] Likely all of these versions make us feel little bit uncomfortable about God's role in the provoking element here. Perhaps one way to think of this is, "the heart of God that wanted David aware of the relative values of having faith in God and not in others awakened the part of David that put faith in material possessions and numbers." Joab tries to warn against this census but David persists. No sooner is he done than he realizes that the census was not such a good idea. This time David realizes the mistake before God calls him on it or a prophet can tell him. Nonetheless, God does send his prophet Gad to David for him to choose one of three consequences for the senseless census. It is the classic choice of threes: three years of famine, or three months of running from his enemies, or three days of an epidemic like the plague. On the one hand, most of us might wish to choose the shortest duration of suffering. After all, how harsh can an epidemic be. Still three months of running from his enemies does not put his country at risk, unlike the other two. This seems especially true since David is used to being on the run. This is his first sign of aging in that he no longer wants to be on the run, unlike his younger years when he could handle this with ease. Keep in mind that he will live less than two chapters following this. Is this a sign of selfishness on David's part, just as taking the census was an egotistical pride factor? Is this a sign of lack of trust on his part? Could he not recall how God had protected David from his enemies for much longer stretches in the past? We will never know exactly what possessed David to make his choice after the senseless census. What we do see once again is David's recognition immediately of his wrong doing and wishing to make amends. When David saw the angel who was striking down the people he said to the Lord, "I have sinned; I, the shepherd have done wrong. These are but sheep. What have they done? Let your hand follow me and my family." [II Samuel 24:17 NIV] Here we have until the end David holding out his image of the shepherd and the people, as the sheep. He is the protector no matter what has happened to them. Perhaps this is some of the heart of God.

Some of the symbols that may capture or represent a portion of the heart of God in David are not fully realized until after his death. The Ark of the covenant is one such symbols that plays a substantial role for David even after his death. It will be associated with death but it will save somebody's life who was involved in a conspiracy against the king. The significance of the ark carrying the original Ten Commandments is interesting because David will manage to violate virtually all of them in one act of adultery with Bathsheba as we have detailed elsewhere. Yet he respects the Ark and what it represents in terms of symbolism and power more than those 10 Commandments and sometimes even God himself. For instance in David's first recorded encounter with the ark, he takes 30,000 men who seem to have no other purpose but to transport it. They were celebrating along the way. Then the oxen carrying the cart stumble and one of the men carrying the Ark reaches out to steady the Ark. He is killed instantly. David is instantly angered at God. He abandons the Ark in fear. What is David afraid of and why is he angry? Is he afraid of a God that may be portable but does not need to be steadied by any human hand? Is he upset because he lost a man who was carrying a trophy for the successful warrior king David? Was he upset because he had to stop dancing?

Let's turn to the second encounter. Three months pass and the household where the Ark has been left comes to be very blessed. This is motivation for David to move the Ark. Cautiously he moves it 6 feet. No damage. No loss of life. He begins the celebration all over. We have detailed this elsewhere as to what happens when his wife Michal complains that he was inappropriate. Perhaps one of David's rationalizations to her was "hey, God wasn't upset with dancing this time, so probably wasn't the last time, so what's your problem?" So for David the Ark has come to represent a power to destroy that he does not understand as well as a power to bless that he can appreciate. Enter the third encounter when he is on the run from the revolting Absolom in Second Samuel chapter 16. The priests have fled the city with David along with the Ark. Up until this point David had not consulted God since well before one of his sons raped one of his daughters and subsequently a second son killed the rapist while David did nothing. Now while on the run he sends the Ark back to the royal city with the following statement.... "If I find favor in the Lord's eyes, he will bring me back and let me see it and his dwelling place again. But if he says I am not pleased with you, then I am ready; let him do to me whatever seems good to him". [II Samuel 15:25-26] In so doing David is using the Ark as an omen, literally a divine divining rod. He is one win with the Ark and one loss. On the other hand David seems humbled and maybe even penitent. We would like to believe. But his language is let him do whatever seems good to him. David, let us clarify for you. God does not need your permission to act. He does not need your definition of what "seems " good. That's a bit disingenuous. Does he not trust that all that God does in the long run is Good? Is he trying to mimic Abraham's challenge to God over the bargain for Sodom and Gomorrah, " shall not the judge of all the earth do right?" Up to this point David still hasn't prayed to God.

But he is almost ready to pray to God for the first time in a long time. He is on the run from a capable adversary. What does he pray for? What we all would in some fashion. For bad counsel to come to his enemy. So what actually happens. The main advisor that both David and Absolom respect is Ahithophel. His first recorded advice to Absolom is for him to sleep with David's concubines. " Then all Israel will hear that you have made yourself a stench in your father's nostrils, and the hands of everyone with you will be strengthened" [II Samuel 16.21 NIV]. Was this advisor correct? Well turn to verse 23 for that answer. "Now in those days the advice Ahithophel gave was like that of one who inquires of God. That was how both David and Absolom regarded all of Ahithophel's advice." [II Samuel 16 NIV]. Despite this Absolom does not listen to his next advice to attack. Rather he listens to David's spy and does not. The result is disastrous. David may survive, but it is not because it happened as he prayed for. Fast forward to First Kings where David is dying. His son Adonijah has a revolt. It involves Joab, David's key general and the priest Abiathar. Adonijah and Joab will both die for their efforts. Though Solomon says Abiathar deserves to die, he will not be put to death but merely demoted because he carried the Ark of God and shared in David's hardships. Second Kings 2:26.

We see through all this the tremendous power of the Ark and the respect that David has even when he does not understand its power. He learns somehow that you cannot try to tell God where he can reside. He learns that God does not need his help to steady the Ark. He appears to have this respect passed on tho his son Solomon who is the next king as he will let an insurrectionist live because of their history of connection with the Ark. Would David have fared better if he had incorporated the contents of the Ark, namely the 10 Commandments?

Of course God can use David, even with his imperfections. Unlike Michelangelo who covers over David's imperfections, God does not want to cover up these imperfections, but presents them and all their flaws and then purifies them, sometimes with some strong consequences. While there is the death of the first born child of David and Bathsheba, the second born, is Solomon who goes on to reign for many years following David's death. Solomon brings an additional element of God's wisdom and peace that David did not have in his lifetime; in fact, we may recall that David was unable to make a temple for God as his home because of the fact he was very much a warrior king and not a man of peace. [II Samuel 7] This is a part of the continuity theme, which is a very important theme for David throughout much of his lifetime.

Having the security pledge and throne that David established forever is a big thing for David. Virtually every version of II Samuel 7:11-16 has mention of the forever clause. Some versions mention that several times while The Message tries to put a check on some of that and mention it only once. David runs with this a long ways and emphasizes the forever clause several times, in different ways, depending on the version. David does the humble routine quite well while mixing in his plug about the continuity for eternity clause, "And if this were not enough in your sight sovereign Lord, you have also spoken about the future of the house of your servant. . . [II Samuel 7:19 NIV] Then, after some more laudatory remarks from God he has David say, "You have established for yourself your people Israel as your very own forever, and you, O Lord have become their God." [II Samuel 7:24 ERV]

But, this is not enough for David who has to have three more assurances in the next paragraph and 2-3 more in the rest of the chapter. "And now Lord God keep forever this promise you have made concerning your servant and his house. Do as you promised so that your name will be great forever and then men will say, 'The Lord God Almighty is God over Israel! And the house of your servant David will be established before you'!" [II Samuel 7:25-26 NIV] In one paragraph David has gone from being most humble to most needy to hear God's promises several times. But, in this paragraph there is a subtle twist. It is as though God almost needs David and his offspring to have his own name be great. "Do as you promised so that your name will be great forever." Reframed from another perspective: "if you don't keep your promises God, your name will not be necessarily great among men."

We must keep in mind that while David ultimately wants the security pledge from God about the continuity, that he also likes hearing from humans. Arguably, this is one of the additional factors that attracts him to Abigail while she is still married to Nabal. We recall her words, "Please forgive the transgression of your handmaiden, for the Lord shall establish a lasting dynasty for my Lord, because your lordship is fighting the battles of the Lord and there is no evil to be found in you your whole life long." [I Samuel 25] This is quite a statement encompassed in one verse, but certainly appears to have an appeal to David because of that forever concept. Obviously, the house of David does not continue in this exact fashion or literally any more than David did not sin for the rest of his life This means of course that we must reconcile that either;

1. She is lying.
2. There is a misquote.
3. She is speaking with analogies.

Those that follow the New Testament will favor the analogy role while other interpretations could also exist by that knowledge. David seems to enjoy this combination of God and women as part of his continuity/forever clause knowing that he needs both somehow in order to pull that off.

David is indeed filled with a mixture of images that clearly represent some of the heart of God through those images, some that might point to that image and others which are questionable images. Recall that the immediate precursor to the senseless census to David's soliloquy in chapters 22 and 23 of II Samuel. Keep in mind that chapter 23 is giving the prefaced as the last words of David. In chapter 22 we have the egotistical side of David virtually claiming perfection.

> The Lord rewards me because I do what is right;
> He blesses me because I am innocent.
> I have obeyed the law of the Lord;

I have not turned away from my God.
I have observed all of his laws;
I have not disobeyed his commands.
He knows that I am faultless,
But I have kept myself from doing wrong.
And so he rewards me because I do what is right,
Because he knows I am innocent.
[II Samuel 22:21-25 GNB]

He goes on to tell how much he has been blessed and how his enemies have been subdued because of God's blessing, etc. He winds this speech down in chapter 23 with what are listed as his last words. We will return to those words in a moment. For now I wish to highlight an unusual contender for God's heart in David: transparency. As we mentioned earlier, someone in David's court may well have authored these works, perhaps with David's recognition, permission, and encouragement. As such, we must give credit to David for transmitting or allowing to be transmitted the essential elements of his life that are not so sanitized. This bravagado of perfection is, as you may recall, followed by the senseless census as though his ego knew no bounds.

Regardless of how he sees himself as perfect, despite his many and obvious flaws, we must agree that to a fair sense that David rightfully sees himself as blessed. This is evident several times throughout his life, outside of his closing soliloquy. Still his manifesto is captured concisely in his closing soliloquy. [II Samuel 23]

And that is how God will bless my decedents,
Because he has made an eternal covenant with me,
An agreement that will not be broken,
A promise that will not be changed.
That is all I desire;

That will be my victory
And God will surely bring it about.
[II Samuel 23:5 GNB]

That is ultimately where David's heart lies at the end of his life. It lies in recognition that he has been blessed by God, and that he has an eternal covenant that will last for his family. That desire referenced exceeds all of his hormonal desires. It exceeds all of his battle victories. It ties his family together across generations that he could not bring about in his life. It is an image that is only through looking at David through multiple images.

Christ Symbolism

ADDENDUM: In this portion we will expand on the eight traits referenced in this chapter, which ostensibly apply to Christ but are actually applicable to Uriah.

Presumably the loyal general Uriah must die because he stands in the way of David's more important conquest of women. At first reading this is the story of a cuckolded man for whom a king wants to get to accept paternity for a child fostered illegitimately by the king through Uriah's wife, Bathsheba. The story is so well known that we can't readily conceive of more to it even though we have significant contempt for the perpetrator, David, who in most other settings appears to be a hero. We know the basics. David has desires for Bathsheba, then intimacy, then word of pregnancy. When Uriah refuses subsequently to have intimacy with his wife during a time of war, he foils David's paternity blame attempt and must die. The summary in a nutshell of the legacy of Uriah seems to be that he disobeyed the king David and that he must die because he did not have sex with his wife. It's all right there. David commands Uriah to go home and spend some time with his wife, but Uriah refuses.

While David never mentions that Uriah should enjoy some intimacy with his wife, Uriah very much understands what the plan was even if he does not know why. In verse 11 of second Samuel chapter 11 Uriah notes that he would not do anything like that as long as David lived. David even sends spies to try to verify that Uriah would follow through, but he disappoints. Next David attempts to get this honorable man drunk in order to do the deed. Uriah may well have been totally drunk, but he does not succumb to David's deceitful plan.

The stage then is fully set and we have only to play out the last tragic scene in which Uriah must die. He must not just die though. He must die a most dishonorable death in which his fellow soldiers retreat behind him and leave him defenseless. That, believe it or not, is not the most ignominious aspect of the whole process. Rather, there is a setup such that his legacy will be tarnished forever and a day. Read again the discussion that the messengers are to give David when they give him the news of Uriah's death in second Samuel chapter 11 versus 20-21. At first glance this appears to be code talk for the messengers who might not really know what is going on. Verse 21 appears to be thrown in as an innuendo that Uriah's death will be linked to a well known story where a famous warrior died foolishly at the hands of a woman. The loyal general Uriah will be discredited more after his death rather than simply during it by implying that he was also killed at the hands of a woman. Arguably Joab who arranged Uriah's death must ultimately die for this as a witness more so than the allegations mentioned in I Kings. In fact, the messengers may have already known of David's pandering. There were after all, messengers who had to get Bathsheba to the palace to begin with. Then there were the spies. Then there were those involved with the death plot. The circle of conspiracy was widening. Uriah's death is not about paternity. Enough people already knew the real story.

Here's the humbling reality in that Uriah did not die because he disobeyed the king. He did not even die because he refused to have relations with his wife during a time of war. He died because he was a more honorable man than David and David could not stomach the notion that someone might have more honor and integrity than him. Therefore Uriah would have to die.

Read various versions and you will see that Uriah's honor cannot be fully removed since he was referred to as David's servant even after his execution. As noted elsewhere there is a distinct possibility that Uriah would have shown David forgiveness, something else David appears incapable of accepting, an action which would've put David into greater debt to Uriah. (See our section on debt as a tool in which neither David nor his organization could afford to be in debt emotionally, socially, or financially.) While Christians view David as a prototype of the messiah, it is Uriah who in this scenario is the suffering servant, betrayed and ultimately sacrificed by his master. Is Uriah a better prototype candidate? Did David cede his position as a worthy messiah candidate?

While it may be obvious that the eight characteristics mentioned previously in chapter 4 apply to Christ it is not so obvious that they apply to Uriah in the same way. Uriah's death, unlike Christ's, was an unwilling death. Uriah was a scapegoat, not a redeemer. Christ was willing to die albeit terrified, but knew his death would provide redemption. Uriah's death did not bring redemption for David, only condemnation, and certainly no honor.

Which brings up another point. In many ways Uriah's motivations are unclear in the David/ Bathsheba affair. He very well could have known about the event shortly after it started, tipped off by friends and others in David's court. He may also have seen the ruse David was trying to pull off to cover his misdeeds and Uriah decides he was not going to be part of any cover-up that would benefit David or his reputation. So Uriah stands his ground, and maintains his honor. He knew the risks of battle, but a death with honor is better than a compromised life to save or help David's. He did not wish death, but it happens in this scenario, Uriah puts David in Checkmate and brings on Nathan's condemnation message.

Uriah as Scapegoat or a Master in an emotional, spiritual chess game, same result: David's in Check and exposed.

CHAPTER 4 QUESTIONS

1. How hard was it for David to accept the role of humble delivery boy after he had already been an accomplished warrior?
2. What is "the thing" in the Bathsheba affair and its relationship to the Ten Commandments?
3. Why does David need a forever clause and what lengths does he go to secure that?
4. If David is a man after God's heart and yet cannot build God's house because he was a man of war, what does that make of the connection between God and war?
5. What is the most affective symbol for Christ in the story of David?

Epilogue

After hundreds of years of being admired as a nearly perfect sculpture, Michelangelo's David was attacked by a deranged man with a hammer in an act of violence. He struck a blow that effected the feet of the epic statue. For the real David who had been someone who was engaged in frequent violence and acted crazy on occasion, this was ironic. The statue was pieced back together, but the director of the museum Antonio Paolucci said, "The moral impact remains, the world's most famous statue has been damaged." Nonetheless, this senseless act of violence did allow scientists to discover the origins of the statues stone. Meanwhile, most people continue to see the image of David they expect to see.

So, too, has our treatise chipped away at the image of David. We have seen that our hero has clay feet. Like Michelangelo we can see something admirable in many perspectives. But, unlike Michelangelo's statue we cannot admire David from all angles. David is a man of confidence from the very beginning, but his shadow side of the ego will sometimes cause him to do hubristic measures that jeopardize himself, his loved ones, the kingdom, and even God's reputation. David is shrewd and cunning, but his deceptiveness may backfire upon him. He is often aware when confronted and sometimes even before confrontations of the need for more forgiveness from God, but he has a difficult time extending that forgiveness to others. He is a master survivor of life on the run, but when there is a chance to stop great damage to his people by being on the run for a brief time, he declines that opportunity. David's gut instincts may indeed deliver him from many difficulties, but the fear in his gut when he is complacent and not seeking God's vision will cause him to flee when he may not need to. He takes great security in knowing that his family will sit upon the throne forever, but he is quite insecure as to how that will happen. In addition, as much as the family means to him for perpetuity, the immediacy of their relevance may be questioned. At least two of his sons kill brothers while a third one rapes his sister. Whether you are king or a potential one perhaps you perceive the right to take Samuel's warning about the privileges of Kings to its ultimate expression such that even family will pay the price if they are in the way of other family striving for the top. David is often expressive of the many blessings he has, but at the same time can be egotistical in suggesting he has achieved them because he is perfectly blameless.

The expressions of these various traits are achieved in a multitude of roles. His fame comes to us as the warrior hero whose faith is larger than the stature of a giant and larger than the colossal statue representing David. Sometimes he is an example or representation of God's kingdom to other countries for better or worse. He is exemplary of both left brain qualities with his calculating and maneuvering and right brain creativity. He is a musician and poet whose creative works and abilities are able to calm the most troubled individuals. He can masquerade as a priest and a burlesque dancer all in the same scene while justifying each by his rationalization of praising God. David is both lusty and lustful. He is cunning and conniving, but contrite when he needs to be. He can be cold and calculating, but incredibly soothing to other's needs. He is resilient. If necessary he will act crazy in order to achieve his ends. In his own words he is without blame and perfect at times and thus serves as a prototype for God himself or a forerunner of Jesus in the New Testament. Forever David is seen as the good shepherd who will occasionally put his sheep at risk but will do whatever it takes to recover them and provide lasting security.

David's insecurity is most manifest in his need for perpetuity of his linage or permanency on the throne. Symbolism can be used to construe the New Testament Christ as his offspring and reflection of the perpetuity. Indeed, there are multiple ways for David to be conceived as having achieved that perpetuity.

1. Direct descendants.
2. By representation from the court historian who David likely "posed" for and confided all.
3. The Psalms.
4. Symbolism.
5. Michelangelo.

The option not available to David is to have perpetuity represented by a dwelling for God. The man after the heart of God is not able to contain the spirit of God in a building. Just as God did not need David to steady the Ark, so to he cannot be contained by David or owe David anything anymore than David ever wished to owe those who assisted him. Michelangelo may depict an exquisite picture of David from a stone but David cannot contain God in a building of stone. This is despite the fact that it was recognized that David had it in his heart to build a home for God. We must keep in mind that David was unable to build a temple for God despite being a man after God's own heart. In I Chronicles, chapter 22, we are told that this was because David was a man of war, whereas his son Solomon was going to be a man of peace. We see further reference to this in II Chronicle 6, "My father David had it in his heart to build a temple for the name of the Lord, the God of Israel, but the Lord said to my father, David, you did well to have it in your heart to build a temple for my name. Nevertheless you are not the one to build the temple, but your son, your own flesh and blood-he is the one who will build the temple for my name". [II Chronicle 6, verses 7-9, NIV]

This denial may have inspired David to try to leave a legacy and lasting impression through other means. Enter the Psalms to fulfill this drive. David's struggle are reflected regularly in them. The transparency of his weakness and feelings of persecution beyond his coping ability for adversity are all there. His raw utterances give expression for you and I to expose our fears and weaknesses to a God that is not confined to a physical building. The angst that David expresses is that which every human being contains. We see simultaneously that we may well have our own inspired ideas in our heart which must be expressed in some other setting (so too must we all find our way symbolically to express our unique faith in the God that is unique to us).

We may not see the heart of God in all the stories of David, just as we may not admire David from all angles. We may have to overlook some imperfections in order to see the man who once had a heart after God's own image. In our case we began chipping away at the image of David that most of us have had in order to find that heart of David that is a man after God's own heart. In order to have the complete picture of David though, it is necessary that we not discard any of the pieces.

What remains of our image of the heart of God after we have chipped away at David's image? Do we see the heart of God in the warrior hero image? Or taking the solider analogy further, do we see it in David's supreme loyalty? Do we see the heart of God in the ability to sooth even the most afflicted and tormented individuals under the most trying of circumstances? Do we see the heart of God in the transparency, which portrays all of David's images, desirable and otherwise? Do we see the heart of God in the role that David attaches to authority, even if he does not always listen to authority? Do we see the heart of God in the ability of David to discern a larger good and bigger vision, even though he sometimes loses sight of that vision temporarily? Do we see the heart of God in David's abilities to recognize God's many blessings and desires and put them into words accordingly? Do we see the heart of God in David's ability to be resilient and repentant, even after he has committed many blunders?

We must entertain additional possibilities regarding David's heart if we are to find the true meaning of that heart for our own lives today. We cannot escape the conclusion that David dies a broken man, just as his statue was broken many years after it was made. David, after all, dies a tired and vengeful individual with little more than a shadow of his former self. It is quite possible that David died recognizing that much of his life was indeed a sham. In this sense he wrestled with the image he truly was with the image that he could be with God's help. Arguably it is this tension that creates the Psalms. In fact, if one does more than a cursory reading of the Psalms you will find that there is a fair amount of whining and "woe is me" philosophy. Yet this is transparency and arguably one of the reasons that God still used them.

Indeed, it is this transparency that makes us able to approach the shattered image of David. This is the real tension in the image created by Michelangelo that we don't wish to see. Also, Michelangelo's statue is smooth enough that we can almost see our own reflection, but not quite. However, this is arguably the point of David's life in that, as it comes to us and that we are meant to see ourselves in David with all of his flaws and all of his hubris, because, he is after all, also the image of you and me. We recall that in Michelangelo's statue that David is poised to run. This is indeed the story of David's life, whether it involves the heroics of running toward Goliath and other battles with a not so heroic and not so trusting of running away from his own son and hiding when his best friend faces his fatal battle. While it may be tempting to perceive the heart of God as best portrayed in the love that David extended to Jonathan and his family beyond the death of Jonathan, there would be serious challenges to this contention. Therefore, as tempting as it may be to posit the love that David has for Jonathan as an eternal love and thus reflecting the heart of God, we must counter that with the harsh reality that David is missing in action at his good friend's death. Furthermore, it would appear that Jonathan sacrifices far more in his end of the relationship than David does, including his own life and future kingship. On the one hand, David has a broken heart when Jonathan dies, but a case can be made in the closing of his life that he dies a broken man without a heart. In fact, compare and contrast David's death with that which Christ challenged us with. Christ challenges us to die to self in order to be born again. David meanwhile, who serves as forerunner for Christ in many senses dies as himself: cold, lonely, vengeful, and broken. He comes to us in the language of Paul Tillich, a broken myth and it is largely as such that he is useful to us.

If we examine what the purpose of the story of David is or his symbolism without becoming too enmeshed with the idea that the symbol represented by the statue signifies perfection, only then can we reconcile the good of David's life with the less than fulfilled. For a symbol to be useful it must point to something beyond and be stripped of the pretension that it is the perfect reflection of the ultimate meaning of life. David may indeed be a foreshadowing of the Christ or true perfection, but in order to do so he needs to die to self. David, of course, did not sit down and pose for Michelangelo. Arguably, though, David did pose for the court historian, so to speak, who recorded much of David's life-flaws and all. As such he is a broken symbol much along the lines that Paul Tillich describes in his book Dynamics of Faith. This symbolism is still quite useful in that we see even our flawed symbols reflect a certain image of God. It is Michelangelo who depicts David's physical image. It is David himself who projects the heart of God through glimpses in the Psalms etc., but it is God who shows his heart through some of the projections that leave a lasting image.

The beauty of the historical David is that unlike the statue by Michelangelo, his flaws are very much exposed. God can use those flaws to show that even seriously flawed symbols can reflect a certain image of God and point beyond itself. The details of Michelangelo's statue reveal such perfection as does a scrutiny of David's life reveal his fatal flaws. David may well have run as was some custom, stripped into battle, but he is stripped here figuratively speaking for our forensic battle that searched for the heart of God. God is in the details and able to be discovered amidst an imperfect world full of flaws and flawed people. God sees some of himself in each individual after our own illusions have been shattered.

We are no Michelangelo. We are not the first to chip away at David nor will we complete the picture. Just as others started the David project before Michelangelo so too will others come along and finish the project for us. Some will look at this work and see just a crude stone. Others will see something more. Others will look and see in this picture the same stone that David used to kill Goliath and continue to see the admirable warrior hero. Others will see the stones that David's own men were going to use to kill him with his imperfections when they attributed their loses to his strategies. In our title we have the fusion of heart and stone in David and Michelangelo. Sometimes the heart and stone images will come together in David's heart of stone, which he exhibits at times for no glorious image. For example, he has the classic heart of stone when he rejects Michal after her return from the enemy captivation. David also has this heart of stone when he rejects Absalom and the opportunity to fully connect with him.

A rare individual will perhaps see both of these symbols as one in the same along with a fusion of other elements. They will no doubt add to our crude sculpting and make a better picture. David wanted a dynasty that would last forever. We can argue how that dynasty may continue, whether through New Testament lines or through his own Psalms, but we can be sure that whatever does endure must be consistent with the heart of God. After we have shattered the image of David, his moral impact does remain.

We all need a hero. Accordingly, many people will pick up the pieces of our shattered image of David and reconstruct the hero that they wish to see. However, if we are going to have the whole image of David we need all the fragments, including those which don't reflect as well as we would like to. The point is that God still uses David, even with his imperfections. He doesn't stop him from worshiping, he only readily notes that David is not prepared to worship God on David's terms, because even a good heart after God's own may be a good starting point for something enduring, but it is not by itself enough.

The heart after God's own is that portion of ourselves that remains attracted to God despite our flaws. It recognizes our image of God that is at our core of being, but yet has not achieved perfection in its daily manifestations. The heart points to the perpetuity of opportunity for fulfillment. Our flaws may take us from complete realization of that heart, but the heart brings us back to perfection-God's perfection, not ours. The heart of God seeks its fulfillment in a wide range of symbols that cannot be confined to a building or any one credo. When we look at Michelangelo's David we are made to feel as though we are looking at David himself. As we look at the biblical David we realize that we are looking at ourselves with all of the potential to reflect the heart of God or to reject the cornerstone that redeems us from our deeply embedded and sometimes hidden imperfections. The first time David is a symbol for purity is in I Samuel 13:14. The last time is Michelangelo's David. May these bookends help you find your own angle of inspiration.

Abbreviations for Bible Translations Used

GNB: Good News Bible
MSG: The Message
LB: The Living Bible
NIV: New International Version
KJV: King James Version
RSV: Revised Standard Version